CATERPILLARS
Don't
Fly

JONATHAN PRIDE

WESTBOW
PRESS®
A DIVISION OF THOMAS NELSON
& ZONDERVAN

This book is a work of non-fiction. Unless otherwise noted, the author and the publisher make no explicit guarantees as to the accuracy of the information contained in this book and in some cases, names of people and places have been altered to protect their privacy.

WestBow Press books may be ordered through booksellers or by contacting:

WestBow Press
A Division of Thomas Nelson & Zondervan
1663 Liberty Drive
Bloomington, IN 47403
www.westbowpress.com
1 (866) 928-1240

Because of the dynamic nature of the Internet, any web addresses or links contained in this book may have changed since publication and may no longer be valid. The views expressed in this work are solely those of the author and do not necessarily reflect the views of the publisher, and the publisher hereby disclaims any responsibility for them.

Any people depicted in stock imagery provided by Getty Images are models, and such images are being used for illustrative purposes only. Certain stock imagery © Getty Images.

Scripture taken from the New King James Version. Copyright © 1979, 1980, 1982 by Thomas Nelson, Inc. Used by permission. All rights reserved.

ISBN: 978-1-9736-8933-1 (sc)
ISBN: 978-1-9736-8934-8 (hc)
ISBN: 978-1-9736-8932-4 (e)

Library of Congress Control Number: 2020906947

Print information available on the last page.

WestBow Press rev. date: 04/21/2020

This book is sincerely dedicated
to my Lord and Savior, who always made a way;
to my beautiful Anjel, who helped me find the way;
to my wonderful children, who helped me keep the way;
and to my family and friends, who stood
by me every step of the way.

CONTENTS

INTRODUCTION

CATERPILLARS DON'T FLY.
WHY SHOULD THEY?

Every species on earth endures some form of change and evolution. In each instance, it can be argued that the success and longevity of each of these species rely heavily on how they manage it. A caterpillar's transformation to a butterfly is one of nature's most magnificent occurrences. Few scientists know what occurs within the caterpillar's anatomical state to determine when it begins its transformation. The short answer is that *the caterpillar* determines when it has reached its desired size and strength; then it begins its transformation. I believe the metamorphosis begins on a day when the caterpillar determines it is ready for *more*. I believe the caterpillar asks itself, "Why crawl when I can fly?"

When the caterpillar decides it is ready for its metamorphosis, it stops eating and seeks a place of refuge and peace. This location is usually a twig or tree branch high enough to remove itself from natural threats, like rain and wind, but low enough to remain exposed to predators. It then hangs upside down and spins a silky cocoon, also known as a chrysalis. Within its protective casing, the caterpillar undergoes arguably the most aggressive and radical transformation of any species on earth. This stage of the caterpillar's life cycle is called the pupa.

When observing the pupa phase from the outside, one might assume the caterpillar is resting within its cocoon. However, inside the cocoon, the soon-to-be butterfly is transforming its external and internal appearance to match its true potential. Its tissue, organs, and limbs are evolving to enable it to fly. Its instinct to crawl for food is silenced. Its satisfaction with the world it knew dies. It completely surrenders itself to the old and fully accepts the new. The caterpillar emerges from the chrysalis as a beautiful and majestic butterfly, the entire world within its reach.

Many will argue that caterpillars lack thought and free will. Others will claim that a caterpillar doesn't make a conscious decision to begin the metamorphosis; rather it is just a part of its life cycle. Scientists don't believe there are experiences, situations, or variables that force the caterpillar to look within itself and realize a change is necessary. Perhaps these are the same people who argue against change. I've learned many of the same people who are unwilling to change are the ones who try to rationalize against change. They use phrases like, "This is how I've always done it," and "If it isn't broken, why fix it?" when their status quo is challenged.

It is true—millions of caterpillars die before they begin their transformation. Life gets the better of them. I'm sure millions more die during the pupa phase for myriad reasons. After all, a caterpillar hangs upside down inside a cocoon without the ability to protect itself. Hanging upside down is a sign of complete submission to a process. It's perhaps the most vulnerable position someone or something can be in. It's downright scary. During this phase, a caterpillar surrenders to the world and accepts the short-term outcome in exchange for the long-term gain.

I believe there is a caterpillar in all of us. We are all born with untapped potential. We are all born with an inner voice of reason that argues against the outward voice of experience. We face a world set to see us fail before we ever achieve our goals in life. Even more alarming and disheartening, many of us understand this reality and never choose to enter our own pupa phase. Even after weighing the risks and rewards, some choose to remain idle.

Caterpillars Don't Fly isn't about shaming anyone into accepting change. Nor is it about the life cycle of caterpillars. Rather, this book is about questioning the status quo and pushing toward self-improvement. Sure, life as a caterpillar is comfortable when it's all we've ever known. We are surrounded by caterpillars at home, at work, at church, at school, and in most places we frequent. I'm sure you can name ten people right now who could list a million reasons they might accept a life as a caterpillar instead of risking the metamorphosis required to become a butterfly.

I challenge you to read these pages with an open mind. I will parallel change and transformation in both my personal and professional life. By no means am I an expert on change management. I am not a psychologist, life coach, or therapist. I cannot tell you what you are doing wrong and what I am doing right. All I can do is share what the result has been after I consciously decided to enter my pupa phase. I'm sure I will enter several more pupa phases throughout my life. My goal is to be a butterfly in every facet of life. I hope my story encourages you to do the same.

Caterpillars don't fly. But then again, why should they? Why remain a caterpillar, when we can become butterflies?

Jonathan Pride

1

COURAGE: PAINE MOUNTAIN

I grew up in New York City in a cramped house with two parents and five siblings. My parents were very protective of my siblings and me due to the risks of living in New York. Until my eighteenth birthday, I knew only what my parents allowed me to see. Whenever I witnessed violence at school, at home, or on the streets, my parents would explain that evil exists in the world and that the best way to overcome it is to avoid it and seek God's wisdom for clarity and guidance. I was raised in the church and became a very devout Christian at a young age. I didn't know it then, but I lived a rather comfortable caterpillar life.

Then the events of September 11, 2001, fell upon us, and everything changed. From the fifth-floor window of Port Richmond High School, I watched the World Trade Center fall. Ironically, I was in my Junior Reserve Officer Training Corp (JROTC) homeroom period. I watched with the rest of the world as the horrors of terror invaded the United States mainland. To this point, I understood that there were evil people who did evil things. I was familiar with Columbine, the Oklahoma City bombing, the US embassy bombing in Kenya, and other world events. I remembered a young classmate who was killed in a drive-by shooting just three miles from my house, on Staten Island. I had witnessed my brother getting jumped by two bullies for defending me on the playground in middle school. Evil was always real to me, and even as a youth, I was no stranger to it. However, it wasn't until 9/11 that I realized I would be unsuccessful if I tried to avoid all the dangers of the world.

Something happened in me after 9/11. I knew I was greater than my current state, but I wasn't comfortable enough with myself to accept it. I was an emotional kid from NYC who pounded my chest to others while secretly weeping at night for fear of failure. My brother Matt did me no favors. He was all-American in everything. He stole every bit of the spotlight I ever had. When I ran fast, he ran faster. When I jumped high, he jumped higher. When I scored an A, he tested out of the exam because he was more advanced. I spent my childhood in NYC comparing myself to a kid who had no idea he was my measuring rod. My brother was just a good person; he never outdid me out of spite. His excellence in life had an unintended impact on my success, and instead of rising to the occasion, I often hid away in the shadows.

When I played high school basketball, I was one of the better players on the team. I averaged fifteen points a game and helped put my high school back on the map in the New York basketball circuit. I was selected to serve on the Staten Island All-Star team and was one of two players representing my team. My coach was a big fan of mine. When it came time to honor different players at the end-of-the-season award ceremony, I knew I would receive some form of recognition. My brother played basketball for the same coach but did not have as successful a campaign as I did. This would be my time to stand alone and celebrate my successes. When the coach presented me with a trophy, he publicly acknowledged a mistake he made when ordering it. In disbelief, I looked down at the trophy and saw my brother's name. Even after working my tail off all season, in my coach's mind, I still competed against the memory of my brother's success. I felt defeated.

Growing up, I spent so much time trying to be someone else I didn't even begin to be myself. I didn't know how to even start. I accepted what was given to me, and I never pushed myself to greater heights because I knew no matter what I did, my brother would always be better. So, I stopped trying.

Just like a caterpillar, I scrounged around and took whatever was given. I knew I could be more someday but refused to risk the embarrassment of standing on my own. What's more, I justified my inaction with variables that could easily have gone wrong. I asked questions like, *What if it doesn't work? Why would it be any different next time? What if I fail? What if someone sees that I cannot do it, and I don't get another opportunity?* These are the ways caterpillars question themselves before they submit to the pupa phase. Sure, there is a potentially negative answer to each of those questions. What the caterpillar doesn't see is that the same questions also have positive outcomes. The butterfly is proof. Before a caterpillar undergoes the radical metamorphosis within the chrysalis, it must first believe it is good enough to surrender itself to the process of self-improvement. It must believe it can fly.

When my brother left home to attend the United States Military Academy at West Point, I knew I could no longer hide under the comfortable shade he cast. I knew I would either be exposed as a fraud or begin to shine my own light. Whenever I introduced myself to people who knew Matt, they would ask if I was his brother. I would always say yes. I viewed it as a term of endearment. It wasn't until he left that I realized I am more than my brother's brother. I am my own person. I am Jonathan Pride. I began to stand on my own. I began to speak for myself. I began to believe I could fly. Like a caterpillar prior to the pupa phase, I began to realize the only way I would become more would be to surrender to myself and my fears and allow the world to accept me for me.

I began my pupa phase when I decided to venture down my own path after high school and go to college in Vermont. I was the second youngest to five other siblings. All four of my older siblings went to college in New York. Each of them saw the need to remain close to home—just far enough to experience life but close enough to circle back around home plate if something went wrong. I wasn't going to follow in their footsteps. I knew life had more for me, and I believed I could not fully evolve if I stayed in New York.

I decided to attend Norwich University in Northfield, Vermont, for my undergraduate degree. Norwich is the oldest private military college in the nation. It's basically the little brother to West Point. The irony of my decision to attend Norwich, as opposed to any other school, was that I subconsciously wanted to prove I was just as good as my brother without following him to West Point. It was my first act of defiance against the Jon I used to be. It was a five-hour drive from my parents' house in Staten Island. My decision shocked my family. I was breaking up a good thing by venturing outside the nest. My dad, whom I love and respect very dearly, told me as he drove me to college for arrival day that he doubted I would make it through the rigorous first year at the university because I didn't have the same toughness as my brother. I don't believe he said it to hurt or sway me. I simply think he was basing his judgment and opinion on the only version of me he knew: the caterpillar Jon.

The caterpillar in me could have heeded my father's gloomy words and sought an alternate route. To be honest, I thought about it. I almost told my dad to drive me back to Staten Island, and I would just enroll in a New York school. However, I knew that if I did, I would never forgive myself or live it down. I would never enter the pupa phase if I didn't take this first step—if I didn't surrender myself and hang upside down while I transformed in the cocoon.

I didn't know it then, but my first year at Norwich was my chrysalis. There wasn't one situation that can summarize my evolution during the pupa phase. It was the entire year and experience. And Dad was right: it was a very tough year. I went through stressful situations, I pushed my body and mind in ways I had never been challenged to before, and I missed home. I underwent a radical transformation in the cocoon, and it changed my life forever. I can honestly say with complete certainty that who I am today and everything I stand for as a husband, a father, a leader, a manager, and a man can be traced back to my experiences and the fear I overcame that first year at Norwich.

I remember the exact moment I emerged from the chrysalis as a butterfly in at least one phase of my life. It was April 11, 2004. It occurred on Easter Sunday, while I attended Norwich University. When I was a young child, my parents told me a story about how the sun rejoices every Easter morning as a symbol of praise in reverence of the resurrection of Jesus Christ. The only way to see it is to wake up before sunrise, stare down at your shadow on the ground, and witness the ultimate beauty of God. According to the story, the shadow shakes to symbolize the sun dancing in joy. It is believed to only last for a few seconds, so if you look away, you will miss it. It may sound like an old wives' tale. Some may presume with all certainty that there is no way the sun can rejoice. It doesn't make natural sense. To some, it may just be a matter of superstition, a random belief to give people hope, or fear, or uncertainty about our universe. If I'm being honest, I don't really believe it either.

Ninety-nine percent of the time, I would laugh this theory off as absurd. *Impossible*, I would think. However, on that Sunday morning, the 1 percent prevailed, and my mind was made up. On April 11, 2004, I decided I wanted to see it for myself. My evolution as a man depended upon it. Like I mentioned, I was raised in church. I attended four services a week, with my dad as the minister. I believed in God because I was taught to, but until that morning, I had never experienced the majesty of God for myself. I believed if I witnessed the sun rejoice on Easter Sunday, it would draw me closer to God.

My friends in college thought I was crazy. They never believed I would follow through with it. Vermont, after all, is a mountainous state, and the only way I would be able to see the sun rise was if I climbed the highest mountain. Otherwise, the sun would be up behind the tallest mountain, and by the time it crested the mountain range, it would be too late to see my shadow shake. My professors advised me not to climb a mountain in the dark. Obviously, as a NYC kid with zero hiking experience, there was an inherent danger of something happening to me. In hindsight, it was a crazy idea I shouldn't have attempted.

I selected Paine Mountain. It sat adjacent to the Norwich University campus and provided easy access. Paine wasn't the tallest mountain around, but it was a good compromise. The climb was only 2,384 feet to the peak, and I knew that if I changed my mind, I could easily return to campus. After final preparations, I packed a day bag, dressed for a cold Vermont morning, and left a note for my roommates to let them know where I was going and what time I should return.

I left campus at 3:30 a.m., allowing myself two hours to climb the mountain. Sunrise was scheduled for 6:14 a.m., so I would have about forty-five minutes to spare if everything went according to plan. I was in pretty good shape, and I hoped I wouldn't run into any difficulties if I just stayed on the trail. Temperatures were in the low twenties, so I knew I had to layer my clothes and not get caught underdressed. There were still six inches of snow on the ground, so I took bigger steps at a slower pace in order to conserve my energy. I was terrified. Never in my wildest dreams had I imagined doing something this crazy when I was a kid. I was a caterpillar at heart and never wanted to go against the grain.

I jumped at every sound I heard. I saw plenty of wildlife. Rabbits, deer, and foxes were everywhere. My biggest fear was an encounter with a bear. I was prepared for the smaller animals, but I had no plan for what I would do if I came across a black bear. With every step I took up the mountain, my heart beat faster. I looked back at the campus from each new height and convinced myself I already proved my point. No one believed I would follow through with it. I could've easily stopped at any point and already accomplished more than anyone had given me credit for.

As I climbed, I questioned, *why am I even making this trek?* I mean, what did I really stand to gain? I deliberated with myself on the value of finding the answer. I wondered how I would feel if I climbed this mountain only to find out nothing mysterious happens on Easter morning, that it is just another sunrise. I would've been crushed. I also wondered how I would feel if I made it all the way to the top and witnessed the wonders of God, only to find that no one believed me.

I reached the summit at approximately 5:47 a.m. The sky was an eerie color, and the horizon was lightening by the minute. I had less than thirty minutes until sunrise, and I knew I didn't want to miss it. I said a quick prayer, thanking God for the courage and strength to reach the mountaintop. I took pictures of my milestone and archived it so I wouldn't forget it. Alas, 6:10 a.m. arrived, and I looked toward the horizon. My moment of clarity was at hand. The rays of the sun began to illuminate the horizon. I waited for the sun to emerge so I could finally look down at my shadow.

With this resolute decision, I felt as if I had finally overcome all the fear I had experienced throughout my life: my fear of being alone, my fear of failure, my fear of the unknown, and my fear of mediocrity. There I was, on the top of a mountain by myself, facing the unknown in sub-freezing temperatures, doing something everyone said was crazy and a waste of time and chasing an answer to a question I wasn't even sure was worth answering. I didn't realize until later that the journey was far more important than the destination.

As I looked down at my shadow, I knew my life would never be the same. I emerged from the mountaintop that day with a fresh perspective. Like a brave caterpillar who surrenders to the world as it undergoes the most radical transformation on earth, I surrendered myself to my fears. Before April 11, I was a NYC boy who grew up with five siblings and two parents in a two-bedroom house just above the poverty line. I had no clue what life had to offer because I saw the world through a limited scope. I was a boy who lived in the shadow of a big brother who did no wrong. I was a kid who was told I couldn't survive the rigors of a military school because I wasn't physically and emotionally strong enough. I had no identity. I believed in myself, but I didn't accept myself. I knew I could be more, but I didn't know how I could achieve it.

After April 11, I knew fear was nothing. I knew I could do anything I set my mind to. I knew nothing was impossible and that I was born with unlimited courage, strength, and perseverance. It was up to me to harness it. Most importantly, I learned that with every decision I make as a human, there will be countless others who will stand against me to argue why it can't or shouldn't be done. These are caterpillars who are not yet ready for the pupa phase. I emerged from my chrysalis with wings like a butterfly and knew no height was out of reach. I was ready for a new world and any challenges and opportunities it presented.

Not only did I survive Norwich University, but I graduated with honors as a second lieutenant in the United States Army and promoted into various positions in my military and civilian careers ahead of my peers. I believe that I would have attained none of my achievements in life had I not taken the hike up Paine Mountain- had I not entered into my cocoon. I also believe the mountaintop was the closest I've ever been to God. It was also the closest I've ever been to my true self, alone on a mountaintop while the world slept.

What happened when I saw my shadow? Did the sun rejoice like I had heard and hoped? Was I disappointed with the answer?

Before I answer these questions and reveal whether my journey up the mountain ended in success or failure, I should explain how my decision to even make the journey in the frigid cold gave me all the answers I needed before stepping foot on the mountain. This story is about the transformation and evolution from the old to the new.

Caterpillars don't fly. To achieve a life of fulfillment and success, it is better not to try to fly as a caterpillar. A person should recognize that change must come from within. After doing so, they will aim to find a place or point in life when they are ready, hang upside, and accept the vulnerability of complete surrender. Only then can they emerge a butterfly.

2

DESTINY: JAMES THRASH

The most important realization I've come to in life thus far is that I am not in control. Even when I am, I am not. Most parents will understand exactly what I am saying. The reality is, no matter how hard you push, pull, tug, grind, hustle, and maneuver, there will be forces just beyond your control that can easily undo all the efforts you've made to progress yourself and your situation. I imagine this explains why Reinhold Niebuhr's *Serenity Prayer* is so impactful for millions of people:

> God, grant me the Serenity
> to know the things I cannot change.
> Grant me the Courage
> To change the things I can,
> And grant me the Wisdom
> To know the difference.

Change is such a scary concept because it cannot be controlled. It can be initiated and prompted. It can be tempered. It may even be scripted. But it cannot be controlled. It is uncontrollable because we cannot manipulate how change is perceived. Change management is all about managing expectations and perceptions, not the change itself.

Mark Krivoruchka, a mentor of mine, was giving a leadership and professional development lecture to a group of people and instructed everyone to grab a sheet of paper and draw a big circle. Just outside of the circle, he told everyone to write, "Things completely outside of my control and influence." Just inside the big circle, he asked them to write the words, "Things I cannot control." He then had everyone draw a smaller circle within the big circle and label it, "Sphere of influence." Finally, he instructed the class to draw an even smaller circle and label it, "Things I can control."

As caterpillars, we often see the limitations in the things we cannot control as obstacles that cannot be overcome. For some of us, the gaps between what cannot be controlled and what can be controlled are as wide as the Grand Canyon. Imagine a caterpillar trying to cross the canyon at its widest point. If not impossible, it's at least highly improbable. The odds are stacked against the caterpillar. Now imagine, in the same sense, a butterfly attempting to cross the canyon at the widest point. It undoubtedly becomes a more manageable feat. Sure, the journey will be difficult with the crosswinds, risk of predators, and fear of falling. Still the journey seems more plausible.

I challenge you to draw your own circle right now. Instead of labeling the circles as I did in the image below, write *specific* things in *your* circles that fit into those categories. Here are a few examples to get the ball rolling: What is completely outside of your control? *The weather, others' opinions of you, how you are perceived.* What are some things outside of your control? *A counteraction to an action, whether or not you get the promotion even though you are the most qualified, the decisions your kids make as teenagers and young adults even though you've prepared them to the best of your ability.* What/Who is in your sphere of influence? *Your kids, your coworkers, your family, your friends.* What are things you *can* control? *Your ethics, your values, your behaviors, your attitude, your beliefs.*

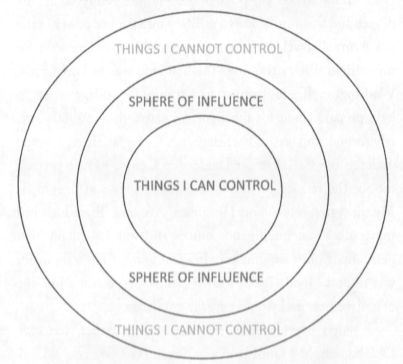

THINGS COMPLETELY OUTSIDE MY CONTROL

THINGS I CANNOT CONTROL

SPHERE OF INFLUENCE

THINGS I CAN CONTROL

SPHERE OF INFLUENCE

THINGS I CANNOT CONTROL

THINGS COMPLETELY OUTSIDE MY CONTROL

When the tiny caterpillar surrenders to the process of metamorphosis, it cannot control what happens to it as it transforms within the cocoon. Outside the safety of the shell, the world is changing, moving, and shaking. Meanwhile, inside the shell, the only struggle is within the caterpillar itself. This is the practical application of transformational leadership. As we encounter each obstacle in life, we will be faced with the decision to address it through the eyes of a caterpillar or a butterfly. I call this *destiny*.

After four amazing years at Norwich University, the time came for me to take my place in the world. Upon receiving my degree and a commission as a military intelligence officer in the US Army, I traveled to three temporary duty assignments for my initial military training. The first stop was to Fort Lewis, Washington. There, I served as a trainer for college cadets to help prepare them for the rigors of active duty military life. My second stop was to Fort Benning, Georgia. There, I would undergo the Basic Officer Leadership Course to help prepare me for the burden of leading America's sons and daughters. My third stop was to Fort Huachuca, Arizona. There I learned my trade as an intelligence officer and was issued my first permanent duty assignment. Ironically, my first assignment was to Fort Hood, Texas. I say it's ironic because as a kid, the one place I swore I would never live is Texas.

I hated everything about Texas. My father, a native Oklahoman, had family roots in Texas. As a young child, my parents drove six children for three days to the Lone Star State to see my father's family. One of the pit-stops along the way was Wichita Falls, Texas, where the temperature was 117 degrees

Fahrenheit. To say it was miserable would be an understatement. I played in open fields with my siblings in Wichita Falls, where I saw grasshoppers the size of dollar bills and mosquitoes the size of quarters, not to mention the frequent threat of tornadoes. It's ironic that the one state I swore I'd never live in is the same state I've spent most of my adult life. However, this isn't about Texas. This is about James Thrash.

James Thrash was the tree branch upon which I began my second pupa. As a young butterfly, fresh from four successful years of college, I found myself reverting into life as a caterpillar. College was fun. The three temporary military assignments I had were fun. Life, up to this point, was fun. Why would anyone want to leave a fun life behind?

During each assignment, I spent the day training with young officers my age. Our training usually consisted of some form of physical training in the morning, work during the day, alcohol-filled escapades at night, then repeat the next day. I made lifelong friends during each phase of my early military career. I also made lasting memories doing things I only dreamed of as a kid. I knew at some point things would normalize, and I would have to embrace a change. I couldn't grow and mature living that lifestyle. To become the person God destined me to be, I would have to relocate to the one place I liked least and start my life as a young military officer.

I remember the day vividly. Shortly after graduating from the Military Intelligence Officer Basic Course in Fort Huachuca on January 25, 2008, my buddy John Meehan and I caravanned from Arizona to Fort Hood, Texas. We had twenty-four hours to report to our first permanent military assignment, and we decided it best to follow each other along Interstate 10 so we could end up in the same unit. Most of my peers in training took off on a long weekend after graduation, but John and I agreed to take time off after we arrived at our unit. After all, our time in Arizona was done, and we were both twenty-one-year-old kids ready to start life in the army.

Both John and I wanted to become platoon leaders for our first official jobs in the new unit. The title of platoon leader is highly coveted for young military officers because it is considered a key developmental position (KD) and can help fast-track someone through the ranks of promotion. It is even more coveted in the military intelligence corps because there are fewer platoon leader positions available due to the military organizational structure.

When we arrived at Fort Hood, John and I walked around the headquarters building trying to find someone who could tell us to which units we were assigned, and in which positions we would serve. It seemed like we walked the entire building several times over before we finally found the person who had the information we both so eagerly sought. As destiny would have it, both John and I were double-booked in the same role and assigned as platoon leader to a military intelligence unit. Problem was, the double booking was a mistake, and only one of us would be awarded the position. So, the question became: which one of us would get it? The decision rested squarely on the shoulders of Captain James Thrash.

It is my belief that anyone who has lived through different phases of life can trace their current situation back to a single event or sequence of events. Some may not remember. Some may choose to forget. Some may not even be able to differentiate between the two. However, I wholeheartedly believe my life today is a direct result of my first encounter with James Thrash in January 2008.

Arriving as friends, once John and I sat down to speak with Captain Thrash, we immediately became competitors. James explained the situation and how only one platoon leader position was available, and both John and I had to interview for it. The person who wasn't selected would serve as his executive officer and thus wait for the next platoon leader position to open in about eighteen months or longer. The craziest part was that the interviews were to take place immediately. No preparations. No interview tips. No rehearsals. No guidance on what traits were sought or criteria on what would get either of us the position.

John interviewed first. I was brought into a small conference room and instructed to wait. I must have waited in that room for thirty minutes, but it felt like hours. I was terrified. I wondered a million thoughts and experienced every imaginable emotion. I questioned why I chose to caravan with him. I hated myself for not driving solo. I doubted my interview abilities. Up to that point in life, I'd never had to stand apart on my own merits. I had always been part of a team. I wondered how I could explain to a man of authority why I was better suited for a role I knew nothing about and why John should serve as the executive officer.

It was the caterpillar in me, not the butterfly, who lifted its head as I waited rather impatiently in that conference room. I forgot about my trek up Paine Mountain. I forgot about all the things I'd accomplished up to that point on my own. I forgot my identity. It was as if James Thrash would somehow expose me when he had me one-on-one. Fear crippled me.

When John completed his interview and came into the room to grab me, he gave me a look of satisfaction as if he'd sealed the deal. I wasn't upset with him for the look. I was upset with myself for overanalyzing the look shortly before I was to sit with Captain Thrash and state my case. I spent what felt like hours subconsciously addressing absolutely everything I had no control over. It was exhausting. I overworked my mind stressing before I even gave myself a shot.

I walked into the room and sat down with Captain Thrash. He began the interview by explaining his rationale for how he planned to make his selection. Basically, the person he determined was a better leader at that point in life would be selected. He asked me questions about my personality, my definition of leadership, and inquired about my upbringing and worldview. As I made my way through the interview, things became clearer. A timely and inexplicable peace and sense of serenity came over me. I relaxed even further. It went from an interview to a conversation. As I listened and reasoned with him, the same peace I felt on Easter Morning of 2004 returned. It was the same feeling of accomplishment and achievement that filled me as I waited patiently for the sun to rise atop Paine Mountain. It was as if I somehow knew everything would be okay.

What happened next was extremely anticlimactic. After both interviews, John and I waited in the conference room together in awkward silence. James Thrash walked into the room and, without pause or delay, informed John he would serve as his executive officer and informed me I would serve as the platoon leader. He then turned around and walked out. Very little emotion. Very little explanation. Everything was stated as a matter of fact, and both John and I were handed our fate.

In total, the event lasted two hours at most. The fact that James Thrash showed such little emotion goes to show how little this decision mattered to him. He didn't know, or care to know, my struggle. It was just another day at the office for him. Surely, he placed several junior officers in positions before this event, and John and I were just the latest. The moral of the story is simple: once I understood what I could control and what I couldn't, I relied more on what I knew I could do and how I knew to do it.

One of my favorite quotes of all time is from Abraham Lincoln. He said, "Let us have faith that right is might. And in that, let us, to the end, dare to do our duty as we understand it." To me, this means I should set out to control only what I can control and impact my sphere of influence in the best possible way to achieve the desired outcome.

I personally believe God orders a person's steps before birth. Countless scriptures and passages illustrate this principle. The one most telling occurs in the book of Jeremiah 29:11, when God says, "For I know the plans I have for you ... plans to prosper you and not to harm you, plans to give you hope and a future." I didn't receive a moment of clarity on why I was selected to be the platoon leader and why John was not. I'll never know if I truly "won" the position or if John simply "lost" the position. It didn't seem important to me at the time, and it's even less important now. Only in retrospect have I concluded that my encounter with James Thrash was merely a part of God's divine plan in my life.

Within eight months of my selection, I deployed to Iraq for twelve months with my platoon. I previously mentioned platoon leader time is considered a KD assignment. Because I deployed as a platoon leader, I became eligible to interview for other positions in the army. One of those positions was General's Aide. A General's Aide serves as an executive assistant to a General Officer in the United States Army. It is a position of great prestige. Because I had my KD assignment and a combat deployment, I was approached by my commander about interviewing to serve as the General's Aide, also known as Aide-De-Camp, to the Commanding General of the United States Operational Test Command at Fort Hood. Destiny was achieved for me the day James Thrash set in motion a divine sequence of events only God the Almighty could orchestrate. Had I been selected to serve as the executive officer first, none of this would have been made possible.

Destiny is a synonym to *divine intervention*. I believe it is impossible to see past the decisions people make and don't make because it cannot be understood beyond the moment. Steve Jobs once famously said, "You can't connect the dots looking forward; you can only connect them looking backward. So you have to trust that the dots will somehow connect in your future." By fully accepting that God has a plan for my life, I live my life only looking forward. As evidenced by my encounter with Captain Thrash, the dots all connected for me in the rears.

Remaining at Fort Hood to serve as an aide set me down a path to meet my eventual wife. I could've easily overthought my interview in 2008, and it might have altered not only the outcome of the selection but also the outcome of my life. God made people caterpillars at birth with the hope and will to see them through the metamorphosis into becoming butterflies. Still, billions of people will live and die without unlocking their potential. I guess the more important question is, will you be one of them?

3

. . . .

DISCOVERY: JOURNEY
TO THE OCEAN

I recall a time when I watched in awe as a public speaker explained the definition of true value. He began his explanation by holding a crisp $20 bill in the air. He asked the crowd if anyone wanted the $20 bill. Quickly, every hand in the room was raised. After seeing the reaction, he crumbled the bill in the palm of his hands to the point the note was unrecognizable. He then raised his closed fist with the $20 bill inside and asked again if anyone wanted the money. Still, the same amount of people raised their hands. Next, he took the $20 bill and threw it on the ground and grinded his size 12 shoe on the note until the bill appeared smushed and undesirable. He asked again who wanted the $20 bill, and every hand was raised. Finally, he picked the $20 bill up off the ground and straightened it to the best of his ability and neatly ripped the note in half. With two evenly torn pieces, he asked the crowd who wanted the $20 bill. Surprisingly, only a few hands were left raised. He closed the vignette with a simple conclusion: "I started this exercise with everyone wanting the clean, crisp $20 bill. After four phases of alterations and modifications to its outward appearance, only a few of you want it now. You see, this is the definition of true value. No matter what I did to the $20 bill, it never lost its value, regardless how it appeared from the outside."

The same is true of the caterpillar. Regardless of its size, color, habitat, or gender, every caterpillar is born with the natural ability to become a butterfly. The bigger question is this: Will it live up to its potential? The $20 bill in the example above never lost its value. No matter how many times it was torn, crumbled, or folded, it retained its value and remained intact in integrity.

If you are anything like me, you will agree when I say, "I just don't feel like I deserve it." It doesn't matter what your *it* is. It might be a promotion. It might be a bonus. It might be a beautiful home or fancy car. It might be a survival situation in which others perished and you are the lone survivor. I believe caterpillars become butterflies because they realize they don't deserve *not* to become a butterfly. In other words, it is my belief that caterpillars are born with an intrinsic belief they are supposed to achieve their transformation and become a butterfly. If God, the Divine Creator of the Universe, created caterpillars with the desire to become greater, how much more would He plan for us?

I have questioned my success throughout every stage of life. At the end of the day, I am a NYC boy born into a household and situation where the odds were stacked against my success. Many of my friends continued the vicious cycles of their parents even though we were all cut from the same cloth. Doesn't seem fair, does it? I deployed to a region of the world during wartime and survived when others did not. I know people who were killed while deployed in support of Operation Iraqi Freedom while serving beside me, and yet I survived without incident. Doesn't seem fair, does it? I know people who were born with trust funds, wealthy parents, and six-bedroom houses, while others were born homeless, in broken homes, and hungry. Doesn't seem fair. Does it?

Life doesn't seem fair, because life isn't fair. There is no explaining why some people are dealt a difficult hand with few opportunities for success while others are born into dream situations. I believe God, the Great Equalizer, measures all of us according to what we do with our opportunities and not by what opportunities we are afforded. I love the analogy Charles Schultz used in the *Peanuts* comic when he explained how some people are born dogs and others are born hydrants. Regardless of the situations or outcomes, you cannot doubt your value because you don't feel you deserve it. I am worthy. You are worthy. The sooner we accept this, the sooner we'll enter the discovery phase of life.

I remember the exact moment I entered my discovery phase. Discovery, much as you would expect, is an ongoing process that doesn't begin or end with the completion of a phase. On Paine Mountain, I discovered my calling to leave a comfortable life. From James Thrash, I discovered the path I would take. In my discovery phase, I learned how I would take the path. The journey to self-discovery and self-awareness is arduous and sometimes bleak. However, it was in my darkest days when I remembered the simple fact that somewhere, the sun is still shining, even if behind the clouds.

Life as a General's Aide is coveted and respected. It is also extremely difficult. As an aide, I had to live a life for two people: The General and myself. My main responsibility was always knowing the variables and accounting for them. A General Officer in the military is equivalent to a CEO in corporate America. As such, appearance and information were of paramount importance. I had to make sure the General knew exactly what to say, when to say it, and why he was saying it. I was constantly on edge and in a career where life and death are part of the profession. I couldn't afford to make a mistake.

In this role, I often worked sixteen-hour days. Whenever I traveled with the General, I often worked eighteen-hour days. I couldn't shut my mind off until I was positive the next day's activities were fully accounted for. It was in this role that I learned the powerful acronym of CAV: coordinate, anticipate, and verify. CAV was my life. Something as simple as speaking in a middle school to a group of twelve-year-old students required coordination, anticipation, and verification.

Up to this point in life, I had considered myself the master of my own destiny. I did what I wanted. I said what I wanted. I went where I wanted. I had a dynamic social life and a loyal group of friends. As I transitioned into the role of an aide, life changed drastically for me. I was constantly tired. I worked nonstop. I worried endlessly about things I could not control. I put the needs of others before my own. And I never received the credit when things went right. I learned the true value of sacrifice.

Prior to my time as an aide, I needed the recognition. I wanted the trophies, plaques, and medals. I wanted people to know I was involved in something, and I was the reason it was a success. Some call this self-gratification. By nature, I loved proving people wrong, and the only way I knew how to bask in my accomplishments was to boast about them. However, as an aide, it wasn't I who shined, but the General. It wasn't my success that mattered, but his. They weren't my words in the newspapers, they were his. This was a diametrical shift in my life, and I didn't understand until ten years later how it was exactly what I needed.

You see, this is the life of a caterpillar. As much as I believe caterpillars are born with innate aspirations to accomplish their true callings, I also believe they are born with a knowledge of all the things that could go wrong; that somewhere along the path, they might stumble, falter, or fail. What if they pick the wrong branch to hang their cocoon? What if they pick the wrong season? What if they break from the cocoon too soon or too late? What if they resurface from their transformation and they aren't the prettiest butterfly? These are like the thoughts I imagine people all over the world ask themselves daily.

I was a good General's Aide, but at the end of the day, I was just another Captain in the US Army who shared a similar promotion date as my peers. I shared the same experiences as them but with different assignments. My moment of discovery happened during the darkest days of my life.

Driving home after yet another long day in the office, it was raining hard in Killeen, Texas. It must've been close to 7:30 p.m. The road to my house flooded because of the rain, and I knew after driving home countless times in rainy conditions how unsafe it was to take this route. Earlier in the day, I had a good conversation with my best friend, who was also a Captain in the Army. We both graduated from Norwich University and both received a commission in the Army. We both made the same amount of money, and both of us expected our promotions on the same day. The main difference between he and I was that he had an easy assignment and worked six hours a day, and I had a difficult assignment and worked sixteen hours a day. And yet, there we were, getting paid the same amount of money for an unequal amount of work. This was the pay structure throughout the Army. It was no different for me or any other Captain who promoted on the same day as me.

He asked if I wanted to head to Austin, Texas, to visit some bars and do some drinking. It was a trip we had taken many times before. He knew I recently broke up with my long-term girlfriend at the time and that I might be looking for a quick rebound. He didn't know my struggle though. He didn't know how tired I was. How could he? He didn't know that even though it was a Thursday evening and every other unit on base had the following day off for a three-day weekend, my General needed to go to the office on Friday to take care of a few meetings, so I would be working Friday, too. Although my buddy and I got paid the same, we weren't the same.

As I drove home in the rain, I was mentally, physically, and spiritually burned out. I was lonely, depressed, and misunderstood. At least I thought I was. Mentally, I was depleted from my recent breakup with a girl who drained everything from me. I had also just bought my first house with the hope that I would have someone to share it with. I didn't. Physically, I was dealing with excruciating pain in my knee from severe tendonitis, a result of my combat deployment. Spiritually, I recognized that my inner voice was becoming softer and softer to the point I feared I couldn't hear God's voice inside my soul anymore.

I made a turn down the road I knew would undoubtedly be flooded. As I drove, my right foot pressed a little harder on the accelerator. Conditions were hazardous, and speed was the last thing I needed to navigate the flooded road. I did everything I knew to be wrong and unsafe, but I refused to acknowledge it. As I neared the lowest point of the road, I continued to accelerate until I crashed into the rushing water at 50 mph. I don't know what I expected to happen. I believe that subconsciously I had hoped I would lose control of my car and slam it into the ditch. I didn't want to die—at least I didn't think so. I had never experienced those kinds of thoughts before. I was usually calculated and deliberate during my time as an aide. It was extremely uncommon for me to lose control like that. I think I just wanted to get hurt badly enough that it might feel like people remembered I mattered. I hit the water, lost control of my car, and hydroplaned toward a 25-foot tree. My car spun violently out of control. I was completely helpless, and the tree was approaching fast. For a moment, the thought of death crossed my mind. However, almost like a scene in a movie, just before impact, a competing current changed my trajectory and pushed me into a ditch. My car was damaged, but I was unharmed.

In the ditch, alone in my car, I cried uncontrollably. I

questioned and feared how I lost hope so quickly. It was almost as if something came over me, a dark entity. It took over my mind and led me to make an incredibly poor decision. I forgot all the good things I had: a loving family, a beautiful home, a distinguished career, breath in my lungs, money in my account, and food on my table. I experienced a temporary moment of weakness that could have permanently ended all the good. I allowed my current situation to potentially determine my future. This was the lowest point in my life. I knew I was loved, but at this moment, I couldn't feel it. Though I achieved my pupa phase transformation two previous times, the inner caterpillar in me resurfaced and sought its way out.

As a child, I learned a very simple principle of faith: the things that are important to God are also important to Satan. Everything God builds, Satan tries to destroy. It took me many years to realize how the "competing current" that changed the direction of my car from impacting the tree to the ditch was God. I bet if I made that drive a hundred times consecutively and maneuvered my car differently, each time would result in me hitting the tree and killing myself. God allowed me to reach this low point, so I could learn that He alone can provide a way out. I saw the present, but God saw the future. God knew that the same job I tried to escape by deliberately crashing my car would be the same job that later led me to my future wife, the love of my life.

Society is quick to blame the recent spike in suicides on social media. People often devalue the legitimacy of depression and mental health because it may look different in relation to the struggles of their own respective lives. I don't personally agree with suicide. I believe there is always a way out. I believe God can deliver us out of our darkest places, and I experienced His rescue for myself. Having been there in those rushing waters, I do understand why suicide is a thought and a discussion.

Self-doubt is a characteristic of the caterpillar, and there is a caterpillar in everyone. The goal in life shouldn't be to speed the process of transformation but rather to embrace it as it comes. My time as a General's Aide was only part of the process for me during the pupa phase. It was a step in my journey to self-discovery. Once I finally emerged from the ditch, I had a renewed focus. I embraced the challenges I experienced as stepping stones to greatness. More importantly, I learned that life in the military wouldn't completely satisfy me. I knew I wanted to be judged on my merits alone and not on my pay grade or time in service. I wanted to work hard and climb the ranks of whatever organization I was part of based on my efforts. While the military is a time-honored tradition and a great career for some, I learned it wasn't for me.

I remained on active duty for three more years after I served my time as General's Aide. I decided at the seven-year mark to make the transition out of the military and into the civilian sector. At the time of my separation from the military, my wife and I lived in Colorado and had a three-year-old son and a twenty-month-old daughter. We owned our second house, containing five bedrooms and four bathrooms, and well over 3,200 square feet. I'll be honest: the thought of leaving the only job I knew was terrifying. Life in the military was comfortable. Everything from food to housing to uniforms were provided. Leaving such a comfortable life behind could be one of the reasons so many people remain caterpillars. Even after self-discovery, action is required to achieve one's desired end-result. People questioned my decision. My sisters called me stupid. One of the perks of serving as an aide was knowing I could get any dream assignment I wanted in the military. It made me marketable. It helped me stand out from the crowd. However, I knew deep in my core that it wouldn't be enough.

My wife, the rock of my life, stood by me every step of the way. She knew such a move would remove every bit of security we had to this point in life. The job I was offered and accepted was in Newport News, Virginia. My wife, a native of Texas, rarely lived anywhere else but the Lone Star State. She never lived farther than two states away from her parents after our marriage. We were always a short drive away from her childhood home. Asking her to relocate clear across the country was a tall task. Still, she gave me assurances that if we had each other, we would be okay.

After seven years, my young family and I left Fort Carson, Colorado, and the United States Army to head east toward the ocean. We willingly chose to start all over in a place where we knew no one. I didn't know what life had waiting for me, but I knew with the support of my family and a renewed faith in God that we would somehow land on our feet.

4

·················

FAITH: TRIAL BY FIRE

The Apostle Paul defines faith in the book of Hebrews as the "substance of things hoped for and the evidence of things unseen." Faith is one of the strongest forces of the human psyche. In my life experiences, faith was the underlying energy at each point of decision. On Paine Mountain, it took my faith in God to leave the comforts of Norwich University and venture into the darkness of the unknown. Sitting with Captain Thrash, it took faith for me to surrender my fears and expect the best possible outcome. And during my move to Virginia, it took faith to leave the security of military life to begin a career in the civilian sector.

It takes faith for a caterpillar to completely surrender itself while hanging upside-down in the chrysalis. Even afterward, it takes faith for the butterfly to emerge from the pupa phase with a renewed view of life from above. While faith is often forged by fire, its effects are usually recognized long after the actual experience.

When I decided to accept a new job in Newport News,

Virginia, I had only my faith to lean on. There was no guarantee I would be successful. I left the military and took a job as a military contractor. Contracting is a career of faith. I say this because unlike many civilian jobs, a career in government contracting is not a sure thing. In most cases, government contracting requires a period of war and a hope that the government will spend billions of dollars to support the war effort.

The job I took was as a military intelligence instructor and trainer. My job was to build realistic training scenarios and help evaluate the combat readiness of a military unit by hosting the training exercise and grading the unit on its performance. I worked for Cubic Incorporated but was assigned to the Training and Doctrine Command, based out of Fort Eustis, Virginia. The funny thing about my first post-military job is that I didn't know exactly what my job would be.

When I decided to separate from the military, I knew I wanted to be judged on my own merits. I quickly learned that my job with Cubic was basically an extension of my time in the military. My coworkers were all former military members and still spoke the Army jargon. They lived, breathed, and slept the military even though they were completely removed from it. Ultimately, because the culture I transitioned to was so much like the one I left behind, I still wasn't happy in life.

One of the reasons changes are so scary is that even after we muster the courage to decide, there is no guarantee we will achieve the desired outcome. Sometimes, there is a second- and third-order effect that must occur before the desired change is fully realized. This is what makes willful change a less than ideal option.

When I started with Cubic, I simply rejoined the life I tried to leave behind. I assumed my role as a team leader and began organizing my first training event in Fort Bliss, Texas. The job required me to travel for weeks at a time for the duration of the training event. Some exercises took seven days, while others took twenty-one days. It all depended upon the unit's training cycle. My first event lasted twenty-one days. I had roughly four months to plan twenty-one days of military intelligence data to support the training event. If this sounds like an easy job, that's because it was. Most days, I spent hours online while at work. I scrolled Facebook, obtained my real estate license, and worked on professional certifications on the job. I worked eight-hour days and went home at the eighth hour, exactly. I didn't leave a minute sooner or later. The job was exhausting because it didn't challenge me intellectually in the way I felt I needed to be challenged. For many people, this job would have been perfect because it provided more time for the things of life which mattered most, like family and hobbies.

Family and hobbies were important to me as well. However, when I decided to risk everything to obtain a more fulfilling life by leaving the military, I never thought I'd leave one job which didn't fulfill me only to step into another. To me, it wasn't a matter of being successful in this role; it was more a matter of being successful in life.

Francis Chan once said, "Our greatest fear in life shouldn't be of failure but succeeding at things that don't matter." My internal struggle wasn't a sense of unhappiness with my current state. It was more of a struggle with the acceptance of it. I couldn't accept it, but I knew I had put my family through enough, and I didn't want to strain my marriage by seeking another change.

I decided with my wife in 2013 to leave the military and start a fulfilling new life. With this decision, we put our faith in the substance of things hoped for and the evidence of things unseen. Like most things in life, the big, bold move didn't go as planned. We were in a new city, with a new job and a new environment—but the same outcome: an unfulfilled life. Not only did I not like my new job, my wife hated Newport News. The faith we showed to journey to the ocean was tested by fire. For the first time in our young marriage, we questioned our decision and pondered aloud if we had made a mistake. Our marriage faced a serious strain.

Things got worse for us on my twenty-ninth birthday. On August 7, 2014, my boss called me into a conference room and asked me to have a seat. With no prior knowledge about the reason for the meeting, my boss informed me that Cubic, Inc., had lost their government contract. Basically, when big government contractors bid on jobs, they are usually awarded contracts that last two to three years, with early termination clauses. Well, as luck would have it, Cubic's contract expired, and instead of renewing the contract, the government selected another company to award the bid and left Cubic out of the negotiations. To me personally, this meant my employment with Cubic would be terminated effective immediately, as my job no longer existed in Newport News, Virginia.

It is not uncommon for government contract employees

to have been employed by several different companies in the same role. As part of my termination from Cubic, I was offered an opportunity to interview for the same job with a different company. As with any interview, I would have to negotiate the salary and hours. Nothing was guaranteed. Even if I did get offered the same job with a new company, there was no guarantee the same thing wouldn't happen again in weeks, months, or years.

My wife and I deliberated the options we faced at the dining table. She was unhappy in Virginia. I was unhappy with my job. We were both unhappy about the uncertainty of life as a contractor. We questioned seriously if we should muster whatever funds we had available and move back to Texas to be closer to her family and security net. It was a humbling experience and a major failure in my first swing at post-military life. Nothing worries a caterpillar more than the thought of failure. The caterpillar in both of us resurfaced and the doubts of life came roaring at us like a mighty tide.

After serious discussion, my wife and I decided it was best for me to interview for my job and concurrently begin searching for the next career opportunity. We agreed to give Virginia one more chance, and if nothing became available, we would move back to Texas. ThreatTec, LLC, became my new employer, and they managed to keep my salary the same. All was not lost. After approximately six weeks with ThreatTec, I interviewed with Mobile Mini, Inc., to become a branch manager in Richmond, Virginia. After several interviews, I was offered the job and began my transition into true Corporate America;

leaving the military behind once and for all. We moved to Richmond three months later and left Newport News behind.

It appeared things worked out for the better. My faith to withstand the fire produced a favorable result. There is, however, way more to the story. Naturally, Cubic losing their contract impacted so much more than just my life and employment. What happened as a result is just as unbelievable as it is magical. Several times in my life, I've witnessed the mercy and grace of God. This experience was probably the most obvious.

When I was offered a position with Cubic in February 2014, it was only made possible because a former employee whose position I filled vacated the slot because he was called to an active duty deployment. He was in the Virginia National Guard and had to deploy to the Horn of Africa as part of his assignment. The way the law is written, a deploying soldier cannot be terminated because of federal service and upon return from duty must be afforded a position like the one they held prior to deploying. When the former employee deployed, he was employed by Cubic in Newport News, Virginia. As such, Cubic owed him a position in Newport News whenever he returned, regardless of whether his job was available or not. Since Cubic lost the contract and no longer had a presence in Newport News, his job was no longer available for him in Newport News upon his return. Resuming employment with Cubic would have required him to relocate to another city where Cubic had a position available.

Turns out, the same day I was offered a job with Mobile Mini, his six-month deployment ended. Instead of coming back to unemployment and uncertainty, he was able to return from the combat deployment to the job I held. The only difference to him was the company who paid him. This is the epitome of faith.

God wasn't just testing me in this difficult six-month season. He also tested this former employee. I cannot fathom the fear, worry, and concern he had as he prepared to return to the United States without a job. The financial burden must have been unbearable. I imagine his family spent many nights in prayer.

As the Apostle Paul wrote about faith, it is the substance of things hoped for and evidence of things unseen. I believe the *substance* was the job. I hoped for a new job which would satisfy and fulfill me in ways Cubic and ThreatTec could not. For him, the *substance* was having the same job available upon his return from deployment. In both instances, *faith* meant different things to him and to me. Even though we never met, it appeared our faith intersected in a way only the Almighty could orchestrate. As it turned out both of our journeys through life shared a symbiotic relationship, even without our own individual knowledge of its existence.

5

······················

GROWTH: FROM BARS
TO BOARDS

Several factors define success when transitioning between
career industries. Timing is probably the most important.
And while timing is never ideal, the right opportunity must
present itself at the right moment with the right conditions to
support it. Otherwise, failure is the likely result. Other factors
include skill-versus-will, personal values, the capacity to learn
the new industry, willingness to adapt, understanding time
commitments, and managing competing interests.

I believe career transitions are the third scariest event in life,
with the first being marriage, and the second being procreation.
I knew I wanted a career in corporate America, but if I would've
been asked to define what that meant at the time of my decision,
I am certain I would not have been able to answer. For anyone,
change can be scary, but when you factor in the journey into the
unknown, the level of risk increases exponentially.

I will not go as far to say the military was a pedestrian life to me, but I can say it wasn't the most difficult job I've had in life. While in the military, I worked with people from all walks of life- Black, Caucasian, Hispanic, Asian, tall, short, fat, skinny, atheist, religious, happy, sad, angry, content, and indifferent. You pick the adjective, and I can name you a person in the military with the characteristic. In my opinion, the main advantage of a career in the military is the knowledge that in three years, you probably won't work with the same people. You see, the military has a policy which requires individuals to make a permanent change of station every two to three years. This was my favorite aspect of the military, because it allowed for a clean start. It seemed that regardless of what issues or challenges I faced, I knew that at a set time, things would reset, and I could start anew. This was especially beneficial when I had a challenging manager or leader. No matter how good or bad they were, they or I would be replaced in time.

Industries outside of the military do not share the same process. It is not uncommon for people to work for many years in the same role and be completely content with it. My beloved mother worked the same job with the City of New York for forty years before she retired. She had the same bosses, coworkers, and peers throughout her time of employment with NYC. I walked into my new role with Mobile Mini on October 14, 2014, with employees who had been with the company for months, weeks, years, and even decades. I entered my new position without the slightest clue what I was doing. All things considered, I knew I had to make my mark on the business immediately without being too aggressive or too passive, because the people

I managed may very well be the people I work with for many years to come.

My first act of business as a new manager in a new environment with absolutely zero idea of what I was doing was to establish myself and establish dominance. This is difficult for both caterpillars and butterflies alike. One of the risks of pursuing success is a natural fear of being exposed. Since people often fear they don't deserve their success, they wilt under the pressure of public perception. This explains why some caterpillars never become butterflies. It's also why some butterflies fail to reach their potential and revert to their caterpillar ways.

I knew on day one I had the credentials to lead my seventeen employees, but I also knew if I walked into my new place of employment with a shred of doubt, I would be eaten alive. I believe this is the root cause of organizational failures. I believe most good leaders assume a new role believing they must make an immediate impact by changing something—it doesn't matter what. The thought is to put their stamp on something and champion it so that others can see that they are in charge.

Establishing dominance can be tricky. When I emerged from my previous pupa phases, I knew exactly what I was being led to do each time. On Paine Mountain, I had a calling to step into my own shoes and embrace the world for what it was. I knew my dominance was paramount in making a lasting imprint on the world. After the encounter with Captain Thrash, I knew I would lead America's sons and daughters into combat. My dominance was required because the lives of thirty-one soldiers were in my hands. When my family and I made the move to the ocean, my dominance became clear as I took our future into my own hands. Once the soundness of our decision to move was tested, dominance became evident to me by the ever-present Hand of God.

In each phase of life, I rallied around a singular event and used it to leap into the next phase. I could not do that the same way now. There was no singular event. There was no divinely orchestrated sequence of events. There was no silver bullet or golden moment of clarity. The beauty of growth is it is ongoing. With each passing minute, hour, and day, situations change, and people evolve to deal with their new normal. Some call this evolution. Others call it adaptation. I call it the quest for dominance.

On my first day in the branch, I knew I couldn't exude expertise because I wasn't an expert in the industry. Dominance for me had to come in the form of confidence. Granted, I had no experience in Mobile Mini or in the equipment-rental industry. I did, however, have an unwavering confidence in myself and in my ability to figure it out.

Christopher Miner, a mentor of mine, shared an analogy during my interview for branch manager. I did not realize it then, but the moral of the analogy helped me transition mentally in ways I couldn't have imagined. He started by describing a time when British engineers were attempting to develop a blast-proof windshield for high-speed trains in England. These trains would travel at speeds of more than 120 mph. At times, birds would fall victim to the train and would often crack the windshields.

While searching for ways to mitigate the effect of bird strikes on the high-speed rail, the engineers reached out to American NASA engineers and requested help in finding a solution. They knew NASA was successful in reducing the damage to the space shuttle during the launch into space and, with this added knowledge, might be able to assist them in developing the technology needed to minimize damage to the windshield.

For several months, engineers from both nations exchanged information and technology. Eventually, they reached a solution and all that remained was testing it. The British engineers asked NASA what they should use to test the strength of the improved windshield. NASA recommended taking whole chickens and firing them from cannons at the estimated speed of the rails to see how the windshields held up. Repeatedly, the British engineers fired chickens at the windshield and each attempt resulted in catastrophic loss to the windshield.

Again, the British engineers reached out to the Americans and explained the situation to them. The Americans assured the British that it worked for them during their own testing phase, and if the windshields were designed correctly, it should work for them as well. They attempted again, firing the chickens from the cannon, but it still yielded the same catastrophic result. One more time, the British went to the Americans and requested guidance after several failed attempts. Without knowing what else to recommend, the American engineer asked a simple question to his British counterpart: "Did you thaw the chicken?"

This analogy, whether true or not, is the first step in

establishing dominance. You and I are no different from anyone who has ever transitioned between career fields. The age-old adage of having only one opportunity to make a first impression is true for anyone who makes a career move. I knew confidence would lead to my eventual dominance, but I also knew I had to first thaw the chicken. I couldn't come into my branch hard and cold, pounding an iron fist and barking orders. I also couldn't come into the branch with an olive branch and ask my employees for peace and obedience. There had to be a balance.

The road I chose to take was one of common ground. I understood the only reason I held this new job was because my predecessor had failed. He wasn't promoted or moved laterally; he was fired for negligence and abuse of power. Common ground would be my power play, and the platform I chose was Cracker Barrel. I took my employees to Cracker Barrel and issued a directive to not speak a word about work or Mobile Mini. We started the breakfast with my own introduction; people had to learn who I was. We then went around the room, and I had everyone else give a brief thirty-second introduction and end with their "why." I wanted to hear from each of them the reason why they were working. As a new manager, this was important to understand. Few people work for fun, and even fewer work for free. Understanding why people do what they do is part of thawing the chicken. After the introductions, while we waited for our food, I spent a few moments sharing my vision, mission, and goals.

To end the breakfast meeting, we played the classic game of *two truths and a lie*. In this game, everyone tells two truths and one lie to see if the group can guess which statements are true and which one is the lie. For me, it was a fun way to learn two things about each employee. We laughed hysterically as a team while each employee gave their truths and lies. The breakfast lasted three hours in total. Even with a business to run and time-sensitive container deliveries pending, it was more important for me to establish a baseline with my employees than it was to fulfill our business obligation that day. After everyone's turn ended and the Cracker Barrel staff asked us to leave, we returned to the office with smiles, laughter, and camaraderie brewing.

As I entered the branch to begin my first day of employment, an angry customer waited by the door to inquire into purchasing a container. He didn't know why the branch was closed temporarily, and he didn't know there was a change in leadership. All he knew was the hours of operation on the door didn't reflect the time that we arrived from the restaurant. As he saw us approaching in a caravan of cars, he asked to speak to the manager. I suppose he wanted to voice his displeasure over the lack of service he received. Almost immediately, and without hesitation, all my employees looked over to me and pointed out to the customer with great pride.

"He's our new boss. He's in charge." Mission accomplished. In just three easy hours, I had established my dominance.

I'd like to say everything was smooth sailing after breakfast, but I would be lying. Even after I established dominance, the branch was still broken and needed several changes to be implemented immediately before success could be measured. Without getting into specifics, the biggest and most obvious change was personnel. Even after breaking bread for three hours, I knew everyone who worked for Mobile Mini in Richmond, VA wasn't part of my long-term strategy. Some were poor culture fits. Others were poor hires. I had to develop a plan to get the right people in the right seat on the right bus, all going in the right direction.

The caterpillar in each of us generally tries to find the easiest way out—the path of least resistance. When a threat arises, a caterpillar takes up a defensive position or tries to crawl to safety. Butterflies can evade danger by flying off. Instead of flying far away from the threat, however, they simply fly to a neighboring branch and regroup. Once they assess their situation and weigh risk versus reward, they decide whether the juice is worth the squeeze.

Establishing credibility is almost as important as establishing dominance because anyone can bark the loudest. Dominance can be faked. Credibility cannot. To be taken seriously as a new manager, I had to establish credibility through accountability. This meant I had to terminate my first employee. To be perfectly honest, terminating an employee is the hardest thing I have ever done in my professional career. Even today, I remember the first and last name of everyone I've ever had to terminate. I remember whether they were married or single. I remember whether they had kids or lived alone. I still remember their faces and their expressions when I told them they were no longer employed with the company.

As a young butterfly atop Paine Mountain, I made a vow never to lose this empathy. A lot of what I have accomplished in life has been made possible because another empathetic person met me in my time of need. This is one of the principles of establishing credibility: never lose your humanity.

Workforce turnover and terminations are a vital part of business. Humans, by nature, are complacent beings. Routine creates a sense of security. The feeling of security leads to occasional oversight. Occasional oversight eventually leads to complacency. Complacency leads to lack of productivity, safety concerns, and a mindless approach to a company's overall mission and vision. Every person I had to terminate in the past five years has been a victim of some form of complacency. In each instance, the grievance against the employee, whether safety related or productivity related, was a direct result of the employee trusting things were better than they were. The first person I fired was no different.

Out of respect to him, for the sake of this example, I will call him "Employee X." When I took my team to breakfast on the first day with my new employer, my hope was that all the employees would embrace my positivity and energy. I gave every employee the benefit of the doubt. I chose not to listen to the feedback others gave me. I wanted to form my own opinions based on my own observations. I immediately knew Employee X would be a problem for me. Not only did everyone tell me he would, but I sensed his attitude on my first day. Even still, I wasn't ready to turn my back on him. As I've done on many occasions in life, I approached Employee X as an equal and attempted to leverage the passive dominance I used to win the rest of the team over on day one. Unfortunately, it did not work. Employee X would not be swayed.

After building a case for formal discipline over my first ninety days, it became too risky for me *not* to terminate Employee X. He was taking way too many safety shortcuts, which could have led to personal injury and loss of life. My other employees began gossiping about why I did not address him. They came to me and questioned my motives. They questioned whether I had the fortitude to confront him. They wondered if I would follow through on all the talk about accountability and discipline. Employee X would not change, and I had to make a statement to either act through discipline or silently but boldly, accept the fact that some people will never change. I had to establish credibility, and to do so, I had to part ways with Employee X.

As I sat down with him, my thoughts became jumbled, and my default reaction was to look toward his humanity. I assumed Employee X knew the job wasn't right for him. I assumed he would own his failures like a man and agree the time was right to part ways. I assumed I would lead a conversation in a matter of minutes and agree to walk him out the door with smiles and handshakes. However, this wasn't the case.

Employee X began to cry. He began to reason with me to give him one more chance. He debated the cause of his termination and provided explanation after explanation to defend why the issues at the branch weren't his fault. The more he countered, the more difficult it became. I knew the only way to establish credibility with my team was to part ways with him, but he made it difficult for me. After many minutes of back-and-forth, I told him squarely that we had made our decision, and I asked him to grab his belongings and exit the building. After he left the branch, I immediately called a branch meeting to inform everyone of Employee X's departure and restated my mission, vision, and expectations. If it weren't clear before, it was crystal clear now. Not only did I earn the charge, but I also earned the credibility. Unfortunately, it came at a cost.

Regardless of what anyone tells you, there is a burden of leadership. In business, much as in life, nothing comes for free. My credibility came at the cost of firing someone. Granted, the employee was a poor culture fit and not the right person to help carry the vision forward. He was still a fellow human being, and I struggled with the act of telling another man he no longer had a job. I've met plenty of people in life who don't care about others' wellbeing. I am not one of those people. I care about their wellbeing because I want others to care about mine. Butterflies are majestic creatures. No two are alike. The same is true for people. God created each person with their own purpose and destiny. I have learned to respect each person for who they are.

I wholeheartedly believe we were each created to achieve a certain level of success and that we, not God, prevent it from being realized. It took me weeks to accept that by terminating Employee X, I was doing him a favor by allowing him to move closer to his real calling. Not everyone thinks this way. Some encounter rejection and failure, then blame the world. Others blame themselves and fail to learn from the opportunity that comes with a closed door or the end of chapter.

Years after my first employee termination, I ran into Employee X at a grocery store. He thanked me for making the tough decision to let him go. He explained how much happier he was in life because of it. While the conversation might not have given me the closure I thought I needed immediately, I ultimately received it later. This is how I define the burden of leadership. As caterpillars, we often shy away from the decision point. As butterflies, we embrace it for what it is, make the best with what we have, and lean into the right intention.

Once dominance and credibility are established, the final step in change management is establishing destiny. This can mean many different things to many different people. The *Merriam-Webster Dictionary* defines destiny as "a predetermined course of events often held to be an irresistible power or agency."

The great American march to the West was led with an innate aspiration to achieve Manifest Destiny. The settlers chose to sell everything they owned and journey into the unknown because they believed it was their inalienable right to achieve and attain what they thought to be rightfully theirs. A reckless abandonment of everything they knew in exchange for success on the American frontier was well worth the risk.

The idea of leaping before looking is what brought success to the early American settlers, and it is exactly what brought success to me as a butterfly. At the end of the day, people work for people, not for companies. There have been numerous studies and research projects to identify why high-quality employees leave employers. The resounding answer with each conclusion is leadership. Employees generally ally with leaders who share their worldview. If a leader neglects to relate to their employees, the employees tend to become disgruntled and move on to the next job, where they can find someone to relate to them— or worse, they stay, and the culture turns sour. Humans are creatures of habit and affiliations. Humans will flock in groups with others who are similar in one fashion or another.

When I first took the branch, I knew that after dominance and credibility were established, I needed to find a common goal. The settlers banded together over a shared dream of a new life on a foreign frontier. Sports players may unite because of their underdog status, which then leads their team through a long season and into the championship. Financial experts may rally around the hope of a booming economy. Manufacturers may join forces in pursuit of the perfect product or a solution to a defective one. The medical field may unite to discover a worldwide cure to an outbreak or disease. Everyone is attracted to those who share a common goal. The difference between a good leader and a bad one is what they do with the goal and how they leverage it.

Some leaders threaten a repeat of history. Other leaders coerce people to manipulate them into doing what they want. Still others sell the value proposition. I chose to leverage a form of manifest destiny in my branch. As a leader and manager, I knew my people deserved to be better because we deserved more. I planted a seed and watered it with the sweat of my employees' work ethic to show them more is achieved when more is committed.

Cole Coleman is credited with saying, "I am a great believer in luck. The harder I work, the more of it I seem to have." I took this logic and helped build the dream of a better tomorrow with my employees.

I love the parable of a California farmer in 1870 who owned tens of thousands of acres. As the gold rush made its way to his town, he was eager to get in on the action. The gold was found deep in the mountains overlooking the small town, and he knew if he remained idle, all the gains would be realized by other settlers chasing their dreams. In his mind, his time was now, and he had no hesitation realizing destiny strikes only once, and he needed to act. Without notice or consideration of those around him, he sold his land to a prospector who intended on using it as a staging area for people moving west. The prospector's plan was to divide the land up and build a new town on the land. The sale of the land wasn't discussed between the farmer and his wife. Instead, he made the decision himself and expected his wife and family to accept the outcome of the sale.

The farmer's support channel neither understood nor approved his decision, so they reasoned with him to change his mind. They loved him and wanted to see him happy. At the same time, they knew he was spending too much time chasing a mirage, believing that success was guaranteed in the hills. They weren't even given the opportunity to argue with him. He made his decision and gave the family an ultimatum to follow him west or remain behind. They chose the latter. The farmer took whatever belongings he had left and headed north into the mountains. In his mind, the sacrifice of leaving his family was worth the reward of mining and collecting the troves of gold he heard existed in the mountains.

After two long years of struggling and working the goldmines, the farmer grew discouraged and realized he made a mistake chasing someone else's dream. He knew deep in his core that life was good and fulfilling before he left and that he should have consulted with his family before making such a big decision. With great remorse and humility, the farmer packed his belongings and headed back to his family farm. He hadn't heard from his family in over two years and had no idea where they were or what they had done after his departure. When he arrived back in town, he had returned to a booming California town that had once been his family's land. His family was nowhere to be found.

The farmer accepted a job as a local farmhand working the very land he once owned. A parcel of land was sold to a local family who had just enough land to provide for themselves. The only problem was that with the increase of townspeople, water supplies became scarce. More wells had to be dug. The family instructed the farmer to dig trenches to run a new well. While digging, the farmer noticed a rock that glistened in the sun. Unaware of what the object was, he kept digging, discovering more shiny rocks. After digging for nearly the entire day, the farmer uncovered a massive gold repository beneath the family's land. After two years of struggling to find gold in foreign land and losing everything he loved, the farmer finally realized the immeasurable treasures he sought were always located a mere 20 meters below his feet. Unfortunately, the farmer no longer owned the land, and he, in fact, helped another man chase his own dreams.

The moral of the parable is this: when seeking one's destiny, it's more important to look within first before looking out. Put more simply, don't try to change the world without trying to first change yourself. I knew after achieving dominance and credibility in my new position that I needed to find something attainable for my team which I felt certain they could achieve. It would have been easy for me to point to a specific metric or dataset to hold my team accountable. Instead, I decided to dig below what already existed to unearth metrics the team could work to improve. Continuous improvement was key. I didn't try to hit home runs with every at-bat; instead, I encouraged my team to aim for singles and doubles.

I overcommunicated everything. I used every failure at the branch to teach, educate, and coach. Every mistake was used as a learning opportunity. Every success was a celebration. Every win, a moral victory. The battle to establish destiny required every "soldier" to face down their challenges without fear of reprisal. I picked specific metrics and rallied every employee to contribute to the branch's success by controlling a certain part of the process. It was very possible my approach in establishing destiny could have failed, like the farmer. In hindsight, I could have taken a more data-analytical approach and pushed my team to accomplish more by leveraging my knowledge of financial summaries and profit-and-loss statements. I did not have to seek the *buy-in* from my employees because I was in charge. I was the manager, and I had the power to make whatever statements I wanted to, as long as the results were the same. Instead, I chose to build up my employees and leverage them to launch the branch to new heights.

After one year as branch manager, my branch was stable. Two years in, and my branch had grown 40 percent in profitability. One year after that, my branch nearly doubled in size. Destiny was completed. We transformed a once-struggling branch into one of the top branches in the company. On top of that, on my three-year anniversary with Mobile Mini, I was promoted to Regional Manager for the Central United States and was handed a struggling region with the directive to replicate my efforts.

All things considered; it is important to acknowledge there is a farmer within each of us. Society teaches us happiness and success are measured by things. We are taught that if we are unhappy with our current state, it is up to us to go out and find something that makes us happy. Often, the unintended consequences are rash decisions, fueled by irrationality. Like the farmer, many people blame their failures and personal decisions on God and credit their successes to luck and personal ambition. With each chapter of my life, I have reached a decision point, followed by a period in which I had to live with the results. If the results were good, I credited God. If the results were bad, I blamed myself. In each instance, while I took counsel from those closest to me, I ultimately decided which course I would take. The difference between a caterpillar and a butterfly is what we do at the decision point. Each of us have a destiny. More importantly, each of us are part of others' destinies. The only question is, will we be able to see the results after our personal decisions are made?

Consider the words of Gary G. Schoeniger: "The ability to choose the way we respond to our individual circumstances is perhaps the single most powerful ability we have as human beings." Which will you choose?

Caterpillars aren't made to fly. Butterflies aren't made to crawl. King Solomon wrote one of my favorite scriptures in Proverbs 16:9: "A man's heart plans his way, but the Lord directs his steps." The initial shock I experienced after making a bold move to exit the US Army set me back when I realized I wasn't happy as a government contractor. Like the farmer, I left the military chasing a vision and a dream. When I realized it wasn't what I thought it would be, I decided to trust in God to direct my steps and open the door for me to walk through. The plan God had for me involved my transition from officer bars to corporate boardrooms. I didn't need to go outside of myself to find the tools I needed to be successful. Instead, I borrowed from my own life experiences to empower those around me to accomplish the future God preordained for them.

6

· · · · · · · · · · · · · · · · · ·

PATIENCE:
THE UNFORGIVING MINUTE

The Holy Bible shows us many marvelous ways God communicates with us. Studying the Old Testament, I learned that God used an audible communication style to communicate with His prophets. It was not uncommon for God to have a conversation with the likes of Adam, Moses, Abraham, David, Isaiah, Elijah, and many others. Jesus, God in human form, used parables and analogies to communicate directly to His followers and disciples. His apostles and disciples began to spread the Gospel using firsthand and secondhand stories throughout the Mediterranean to draw others to Christ. After the Resurrection, God sent the Holy Spirit to earth to communicate with humans on a more intimate level from directly within a person's soul. Today, I believe God communicates in ways He knows the person will receive and understand without the fear of overanalysis or doubt.

Some people have dreams, visions, and divine revelations

while they rest at night. Some have extrasensory perceptions and can "feel" when things are wrong. Others are artistic and can see the world as it was created by God, while some have a knack for music and can play any instrument with beauty and mastery. Others can speak many languages fluidly without practice. There are a myriad of spiritual gifts, and God uses each one to address us in the way we can best receive the message.

At just over thirty-four years old, I can recount only two dreams vividly. I can see the dream as clear as day and can remember the words, colors, images, and meaning. This may not seem like a big deal to some, but consider this fact: most psychologists believe the average human dreams anywhere between three to five dreams in any given night. My thirty-four years of life convert to approximately 12,418.25 days. Assuming the average is four dreams a night, I can safely estimate I've had approximately 49,674 dreams in my lifetime. In my opinion, the fact I remember just two dreams is significant.

The first dream I remember happened sometime between my seventh and eighth birthday. At the time of the dream, I had recently been baptized at our church and began asking questions about what it all meant. I didn't fully understand what it meant to be a Christian or even a follower of Jesus. All I remember was that my parents were crying, and the pastor dipped my head underwater and asked me to recite something whenever I resurfaced. I didn't feel any different, and as far as I knew, it was just another church thing people did to feel good about God. I still had questions. I still yearned for a deeper understanding, but at such a young age, I had no idea how to ask for more clarity. I just acknowledged what baptism meant to others and accepted what it *should* mean to me. It was the best I could do with the limited knowledge I had. Sometime after the baptism, I had a dream.

In the dream, I remember dying a natural death and being called to enter a bright light. The light was so glorious and endearing that I was drawn to it like a moth to a flame. As I drew closer to the source, I noticed it was not just any light; it was the sun. I recall looking around on my journey to the sun and seeing the most magnificent stars, planets, asteroids, comets, and colors. The beauty was unimaginable. I didn't want it to end. However, my excitement slowly turned to sadness. I remember briefly looking back toward earth and wondering what would happen to my parents, siblings, friends, and life there. I didn't have many *things* in life, but there were certainly many people I truly loved, and they truly loved me. As I neared the sun, it was as if I passed through a threshold of perfect light and entered the most beautiful place I had ever been. My sadness was gone for good.

As I began walking the streets of this paradise, I recall seeing everything in the most peaceful state. Everyone I encountered had the purest smiles on their faces. Everyone wore white, and the streets were lined with gold. There was no heat or chill. No humidity. No clouds. No sun. There was a natural light that illuminated everything and everyone, as if each person or object I encountered was, in fact, the source of the light. The sounds were so crisp and pure that I cannot find words to describe them. It was almost as if the sounds I heard with my ears were the same sounds I heard in my spirit.

I heard the prettiest voices united in song. It was as if the wind itself was comprised of every voice I heard, and it moved across heaven with ease and without interruption. Every person I met looked familiar. Everyone looked like my father, mother, and siblings. There was no gender. There were no ages. There were no nationalities. Everyone looked the same. They all greeted me like they had waited patiently and peacefully for my return. It was a big "welcome home" party. I wished I could stay there forever. And then, just as quickly as I arrived, I awoke to a dark room with my brother snoring. There was no acrimonious departure. There were no final comments or directions from anyone. I simply was in heaven one moment and awake the next.

The context of the dream is important for several reasons. The first and most obvious reason is the dream provided the clarity I needed as a seven-year-old boy who recently decided to follow Christ. God knew exactly how to communicate with me in a way I understood. I tried sharing the dream with my parents and siblings, but my mortal mind could not do it justice. Even as I write this, my tender eyes are watering while remembering the beauty of a dream I had over twenty-seven years ago with extreme clarity.

The second reason the context is important is because God used the cosmos and science to communicate a message to me. When I was seven years old, I wanted to be an astronaut. I loved space. It intrigued me like no other profession. As a kid, I set up a cheap Walmart telescope in the backyard to count the craters on the moon. It is impossible to see stars in NYC because of the manmade lights that emit from the NYC skyline. It didn't bother me though. I had a natural affinity for the universe, and God used it to show me what heaven would be like. Obviously, I understand my dream wasn't the actual heaven, as no man or woman can see heaven and live to tell about it. The dream and the images of this heavenlike world gave me peace and assurance to believe in God and accept Jesus Christ as my Savior. It calmed my spirit and led me down a path to one day climb Paine Mountain with the intention of witnessing God's Majesty for myself. Once again, the sun would be the focal point on the mountaintop as it was in my dream.

The second dream I remember took place in the same place as the first: outer space. This time, I wasn't a seven-year-old kid searching for confirmation of God's grace through Jesus and baptism. Instead, I was a thirty-one-year-old man facing an internal struggle with exactly what God had planned for my life.

At the time of my second dream, I was busy establishing my destiny at my branch, and things had become routine. I was arguably the best branch manager in the company, and I knew the butterfly in me wouldn't let me rest living life as a caterpillar. I built a dynasty at my branch, and we were achieving every goal I set. Life was good, but I still felt empty. The real difference between the emptiness I felt in the car on that rainy backroad in Texas and the emptiness I felt after succeeding as a branch manager was circumstantially based. When I was a General's Aide, I needed affirmation from everyone to help me calm the storm, and I felt I didn't receive it. When I was a successful branch manager, I had the affirmation from everyone and wanted to be pushed outside of my comfort zone because life had become too mundane. It was no longer enough for me to know I was good enough. I needed to be pushed further.

This very struggle defines the value of patience. In previous life experiences, my impatience was obvious by my willingness to take matters into my own hands. Now, though, my patience to wait for God to open a door revealed my maturity and evolution. The same is true for a caterpillar and butterfly. God never intended for caterpillars to sleep one day on its stomach and rise the next morning with wings. He intended for them to endure great strife and transformation before they could enjoy a purpose-driven life. The caterpillar in us yearns for the life of the butterfly, but we don't often surrender ourselves to the sacrifices required to obtain it.

You could probably name five things about five of your closest friends that you would willingly trade for right now. Maybe it's a nice house, a fancy car, or a beautiful spouse or kids. Maybe it's a location or an occupation. We all have something we are envious of that a friend currently has. I can say this with absolution because we are all jealous, envious, and lustful beings by nature.

I wouldn't say that I grew envious at the time of my second dream, but I would say I grew restless with life because I felt I had accomplished what I set out to and was ready for more. Rudyard Kipling, the author of many esteemed works, such as *The Jungle Book*, wrote the poem "If" in 1895. He wrote it for his son and encouraged him to stay strong through all the hardships life threw his way. The fourth stanza of the poem is by far the single most impactful passage outside of the Bible that I have ever read. I've recited it countless times and referenced it countless more times since I started my growth pupa phase. It reads as follows:

> If you can walk with crowds and keep your virtue,
> Or walk with kings nor lose the common touch;
> If neither foes nor loving friends can hurt you,
> If all men count with you, but none too much;
> If you can fill the unforgiving minute
> With sixty seconds of distance worth run,
> Yours is the Earth, and everything that's in it,
> And which is more, you'll be a Man, my Son.

His instruction to fill the "unforgiving minute" with sixty seconds of distance "worth run" permeates my soul. In other words, make everything count. Make every minute you have on earth the best minute in life. If you can do that, the world and everything in it is yours. This was the problem I had prior to my second dream. I suspect it may be a challenge others face as well. It is difficult to fill every sixty seconds with value when a person surrenders to complacency.

Brian Tracy said, "Success can lead to complacency, and complacency is the greatest enemy of success." The truth is, I grew stale. My life as a branch manager after success stagnated. I needed God to show me a way out, but once again, I didn't know how to ask. I prayed the same prayer many nights during this season of life, and it wasn't until I stopped expecting a response that God disclosed the answer through a dream. We don't always know why God answers some prayers and not others. I do know God is always on time. It may not always jive with my timeline, but He is always there. In every difficult trial I've experienced, God has been constant. He was there on the mountain, He was there in the stream, He was there on my birthday, and He arrived again in the silence.

In my dream, I was aboard a space shuttle, heading for an unknown planet. The captain of the shuttle had a very aggressive but well-respected personality. He would bark orders at the crew, and it wasn't clear if people listened out of fear or respect. Nonetheless, he orchestrated the journey into the unknown with great precision and resolve. The crew consisted of a group of first-time space travelers, and no one seemed to know each other. I was among the crew. There were men and women of all ages aboard our ship, and our mission was to make first contact with an alien race and form a connection. While I do not recall why we were originally selected for the journey, it was evident that each of us brought a certain skill-set.

I looked out the large windows into space and saw many of the same majestic objects from my previous journey into space during my childhood dream. Billions and billions of galaxies were visible as we traveled through the vast unknown. The crew began to make small talk about backgrounds and experiences, and I gradually realized I had crossed paths with each of them at some point in my life. One of the members was my first boss when I worked for the New York Urban League at sixteen years of age. Another was a stranger I helped on the side of the road when I drove from Arizona to Texas after completing my training at Fort Huachuca. Each crew member held a certain level of significance in my life and helped prepare me personally for this journey. The captain was the only face I saw but couldn't recognize. I saw his face structure and his facial features, but I never actually saw his face. It was the strangest thing.

When we embarked upon the planet, the captain yelled for everyone to get ready and reminded everyone why we were there. Our jobs were to separate and collect intelligence and information from the indigenous race and bring it back to the ship to analyze and consolidate. There was no minimum or maximum time requirement. We were instructed to take as long as it took to get the job done.

When I exited the shuttle, I was immediately welcomed by an indigenous person, who grabbed me by the hand and dragged me to the village. The other crew members frowned briefly and exited the spacecraft together. When I arrived at the village, everyone was excited to see me and seemed as if they were waiting for my arrival. Immediately, they began sharing their culture with me and showering me with gifts. The admiration was palpable. In exchange, I celebrated their culture with them and complimented the simple complexity of their society.

It may seem like an oxymoron, but the indigenous people lived the simplest lives, yet understanding the culture took great patience and knowledge. I recall seeing each person living a life of peace, calm, and happiness. There were no worries, no concerns, and no violence or anger. It was as if life as they knew it was complete, and nothing could deter them from their calling. I knew their language, and they knew mine. It was almost as if we were one people separated by different worlds. I dined with them, and they hosted me as if I were a traveling king from a foreign land. I could not have been happier than I was in that moment.

I don't know how long I stayed in the village. It could have been days or years. I do know when it was time for me to return to the ship, the villagers offered to follow me wherever my next stop would be. It didn't matter to them that they were leaving their lives and families and village behind. I built such a rapport in such a short time that I had the love, loyalty, and commitment of this alien race. I explained to them how my mission wasn't to remain there with them but to move on to the next planet to encounter a new set of people. At least that is what I thought my mission would be. So, I gathered my belongings and returned to the ship.

When I returned to the shuttle, it appeared everyone was excited to hear about my time on this planet. The captain hadn't yet arrived, so we had time to talk about our experiences. I went through everything with the crew. I explained how peaceful the indigenous people were and how fulfilling their lives were. I spared no details. The crew was captivated by every word I shared. However, I did not feel that they were captivated by me but by the lives of the alien race. And this was perfectly fine to me. I didn't yearn for attention. I was perfectly content sharing the lives of others without receiving the credit for gathering it. The crew wanted every detail and held on to each experience as if it were their own. In the dream, I couldn't tell if I had more fun spending time with the locals or explaining their lives to my peers. I felt a great sense of accomplishment.

When the captain returned, the mood suddenly changed. I could not understand why. Prior to his return, everyone on the shuttle was talkative, lively, and jovial. After his return, everyone on the shuttle reverted to the way they were before. I didn't want to rock the boat. I knew there was still more to share, but I did not believe it was worth retribution from the captain. I, like my fellow crew members, had reverted to my former self and rode the shuttle back to earth in silence. A fire burned alive in my soul with my newfound knowledge and experiences. It took everything in me to remain silent.

When we finally arrived back to earth, all the crew members had to meet with the man responsible for sponsoring the expedition. I cannot recall his title or power, but he was clearly in charge. The captain went first. He went into the office and closed the door behind him. He may have been in the office for about ten minutes when he quickly stormed out in an uproar upon conclusion of the meeting. The captain sat outside the office and waited for everyone to present their findings. There was a narrow hallway with a set of big windows which led into the person's office. The captain sat in a chair just outside the office, but he could see the room where the crew waited and see the door into the office.

I was the second person to present my findings, behind only the captain. When I walked into the office, the man interrupted me before I could speak. He said something to the effect of, "Jon, I know everything. You did an amazing job on this expedition. You singlehandedly delivered the information we sought after, plus plenty more."

I was stunned he knew so much without speaking to the crew members. He recalled some of the stories I told the crew. I didn't think it was possible the foreign race had shared it with him since there were no means of communication. Surely, the captain didn't share any stories because he wasn't in the room with us when I shared them.

Before I could react to the man's excitement, he informed me that he had heard everything he needed to hear and promoted me to be the captain for the next expedition. I was shocked and speechless. He stood up, shook my hand, and walked me out. I didn't get the opportunity to say a word, but somehow, it was enough to get me promoted. As I departed the office, I walked past the captain and continued down the hallway. Before departing, I glanced back at the captain. He watched angrily through the window as I walked out. The fire in his eyes burned with great intensity and fury. As I walked away, I knew things would never be the same with the crew, the captain, or the man. I was elevated to a greater position based on my credentials alone, without having to say a word to the people who orchestrated it. I began walking to my shuttle, gathered my new crew, and woke up shortly after.

I awoke from the dream even more confused than I was before I had it. *What did any of it mean?* I didn't understand who the dream was intended for. At first swing, I assumed the dream was meant for my wife, who was dealing with a difficult boss who used her for all her strengths, then took all the credit for the success. I shared the dream with her and thought I would have the affirmation I needed. She took the message from the dream and applied it to her job. Even after seeing things improve on her job, I felt the same fire I experienced in the dream burning deep within my soul. I didn't believe it was intended for her after all.

I carried on with my life as a branch manager for many more months without giving additional credence to it. However, my spirit would not rest. Every time someone complained to me about their situation, I tried to apply the lessons from the dream. *Maybe the dream was intended for them*, I thought. Each time I explained it, the fire grew hotter and hotter. Once again, I was given an opportunity to show resolve and patience with God, but I tried explaining the dream with my own understanding and applied it to the wrong people.

I later realized the dream wasn't about exploring the unknowns. It wasn't about space, and it wasn't about contacting an unknown people. The dream was about the value of patience. The indigenous people and crew members served as a microcosm to everything I'd accomplished in life to that point. Almost eighteen months after having the dream, my opportunity came. An opportunity for promotion presented itself. Several executives from Mobile Mini approached me to see if I would be interested in relocating my family to Texas to take a regional role. I never interviewed. I never applied. When the time was right, the door opened for me without me having to knock. Prior to this, I spent many nights in prayer asking God to show me which door to walk through and begging for clarity but to no avail. Before the dream, I began to believe I would settle into life as a branch manager because no other opportunities presented themselves when I thought I needed them. I didn't have patience at the time. God knew. He knew I would keep returning to the well looking for water, but He purposefully held back the water until the time was right.

As in the dream, my boss was not happy about the idea of

me relocating and leaving his team. He did everything he could to discourage me from taking the position and tried everything in his power to get me to change my mind. I believed he was happy for me but also secretly jealous I had received the opportunity. After a very good relationship for three years, my boss used every petty excuse to sever our friendship and build a wall between us. On the last day he and I spent together, I looked back at him on my way to the airport and saw the exact same look on his face that the captain had in my dream.

As I thought back to the dream years later, I remembered why everyone on the crew looked familiar, but the captain wasn't recognizable to me at the time. The captain in my dream had the face of my boss. I didn't draw the parallel at the time of my dream because I wasn't ready to understand. My boss and I were friends. There was a good chance I would not have believed the merits of the dream had God allowed me to see him for who he was. Perhaps I might have even left my job if I knew the same man who hired me would be the man to attempt to keep me from promoting. Therefore, I remembered the features, but not the face. God intended for me to endure more confusion and struggle to truly understand the value of waiting on Him.

The prophet Isaiah made this pretty clear in the Holy Bible when he wrote, "But those who wait on the Lord shall renew their strength; they shall mount up with wings like eagles, they shall run and not be weary, they shall walk and not faint." I waited on the Lord for guidance and direction. Granted, I waited rather impatiently. God met me in my silence and provided the way out like He's done countless times before. I filled my "unforgiving minute with sixty seconds of distance worth run" every day at Mobile Mini. Patience became paramount. The only thing God required of me was to be the best version of myself every minute of every day. When I finally accepted this directive, He opened a door for me to walk through without me even asking. Such is the life of a caterpillar.

Caterpillars aren't born butterflies. Neither are butterflies born caterpillars. The strength of a butterfly is made pure by the sacrifice of the caterpillar. I believe caterpillars close themselves off to the world while they undergo the metamorphosis because they do not want to listen to fellow caterpillars offer alternatives to becoming a butterfly. Otherwise, there would be no reason for the cocoon to be fully sealed. God used two dreams at two different phases of my life to speak with me about His plan. It took me years after both dreams to fully understand the complete meaning of each. Even after my path was revealed, the struggle continued until I emerged from the chrysalis.

God spoke to me by dream, and in both instances, He used the one place He knew would get my full attention: the cosmos. To each person, it will probably be different. As my children grow older, stronger, and wiser each day, I encourage them to be patient and know God is present in the waiting and is ready to give them strength to "fill the unforgiving minute with sixty seconds of distance worth run." And when they've given all they have; the world will be theirs and everything in it.

7

. . . .

LOVE: TO THINE OWN
SELF BE TRUE

Love is the most important and least understood emotion of the human psyche. Many times, we say we love something or someone on any given day. Perhaps it's a love of something simple like coffee and donuts. Perhaps it's a deep love for a spouse, parent, or child. Perhaps it's a love for a job or career. It may even be a love of a destination or location. We often throw the word around to describe a feeling of warmth and affection for a person or an object.

Love can mean different things to different people. For my mother, love meant waking up every morning at 5:00 a.m., making breakfast for six sleeping kids, picking out our clothes, getting us ready for our day at school, making sure the house was in order, and then taking public transportation to her job in Brooklyn, NY. Her daily transportation required a twenty-five-minute bus ride to the Staten Island Ferry, a twenty-seven-minute ferry ride across the NY Harbor, a twenty-four-minute subway ride to downtown Brooklyn, and a ten-minute walk to the office. Twice a day. After she arrived back home, my mother's love directed her to make dinner for her family, send us to take baths and showers, change sheets, tend to her husband, and then wind down. Often, she wouldn't go to bed until 1:00 a.m., only to rise at 5:00 a.m. the next day to do it all over again. As a child, this was the paradigm of love. My mother, in fact, was my first love. She loved my siblings and I so much that she never once asked for something in return for her love. She literally gave up everything to provide. There was no mountain too tall for her, nor valley too low.

It took me many years to fully appreciate the power of a parent's love. As a child, I didn't always understand or agree with the decisions my parents made. I might have even categorized some as cruel. I recall a few times when I thought my parents didn't love me because they wouldn't let me do something or go somewhere. My young, feeble mind wouldn't allow me to see the entire picture because I could not understand. As a parent, I would sacrifice everything to provide for my kids like my mother did for me. I would literally and figuratively give the clothes off my back, shoes off my feet, and food off my table to give them a better life. I would sacrifice my own happiness and contentment to ensure they are happy. Even when I discipline them, it pains me to my core to see tears flow from their precious eyes because I know my intention is meant for their good. These are the values I learned from my mother. This is the definition of love she instilled in me. I imagine there are days my kids feel I don't love them as much as I really do, because a child's mind cannot grasp the full scope of a parent's love. Love is the single most powerful tool a person can use to overcome whatever obstacle they face. God, our Heavenly Father, loved humanity so much that He gave His Son to live a perfect life on earth, but He died a cruel and painful death for our redemption. God loved us so much, He couldn't stand the thought of eternity without us. This is what we call *agape* love.

I believe parents' love for their children is a lesser version of the same agape love God shows to humanity. In my heart of hearts, I believe if given another opportunity to raise six children in a different manner, my mother would somehow find herself on the same bus, ferry, train, and sidewalk with her hope and desire to provide a quality life for my siblings and me. She would do it all again. She *chose* love, and she chose to follow it every day for forty years. In turn, I choose love for my children. I choose to work, to care, and to provide for them to the best of my ability. I will show them the true meaning of love. Like my mother, I won't be slowed by rain, wind, snow, or hail. I may not be able to provide them with the lifestyle they see on television or hear on the radio. I may not have money trees growing in my backyard. But all I have, and all I need, is within me and the choice I make is to love them unconditionally.

Granted, every parent is not willing to struggle like my mother did for us. There are countless examples of parents who willingly sacrifice the needs of their children for their own selfish desires. There are even more stories of kids who somehow went awry even after their parents sacrificed everything for them. In both instances, neutral parties often question how it all became possible given the different sets of circumstances. The answer to both inquiries lies within the matter of choice.

The caterpillar and the butterfly can also help us understand love and the importance of choosing to remain true to one's values.

God loved humanity so much that He gave every person ever born the power to choose for themselves. The choice is simple: Which version of *you* do *you* choose to be? You can be the "you" who taps into your reservoir of potential and evolves into a complete person, or you can be the "you" who settles into the life you were given and accept circumstances for what they are without trying to change course. This is the same choice God gave caterpillars. On one end of the spectrum is a tiny caterpillar looking up to a world where everything is bigger, stronger, faster, prettier, and more substantial. On the other end is a butterfly with majestic wings, vibrant colors, and the ability to reach any height imaginable. The only difference between the caterpillar and the butterfly is the decision. The decision point is love. How much did the caterpillar love itself to make the decision to become a butterfly?

To take it a step further, the only difference between us as a caterpillar and us as a butterfly is the choices we made, make, and will make. I ask, do we love ourselves enough to make the decision to become who we were designed to be? It starts by holding ourselves accountable.

William Shakespeare put it best in *Hamlet* when he wrote, "This above all: to thine own self be true, and it must follow, as the night the day, thou canst not then be false to any man." Shakespeare wasn't talking about being true to our friends, family, coworkers, or strangers. He meant *be true to yourself.* Once we achieve that, then and only then can we be true to our friends, family, coworkers, and strangers. My mother loved my siblings and me so much because she first loved herself. Only then was she able to be true to me.

I believe life was never intended to be lived in a silo. In other words, life is better in groups. In my pivotal experiences in life, I've had the fortune of starting each journey on the strength of others. Even when I was alone, like on Paine Mountain, the love and support of those who cared about me gave me comfort to know I was not alone in the struggle. I credit my individual successes to those who stood beside me. Life is hard. It's even harder when one stands alone.

Consider this practical exercise: Take a sheet of paper and write the names of your five closest friends, family, or associates. These should be the people who know the most about you. They could be friends or foes, just as long as they are the five closest people to you relationally. Next, draw four vertical lines (make a table with four columns; see example below). On the first column, list each person's best quality (only one attribute). Try not to make it superficial. The exercise will have a deeper meaning to you if you are intentionally thoughtful, and if they are truly the closest people to you, it should be the first thing to enter your mind when thinking about this person.

On the second column, list each person's least desirable quality. Again, only one attribute. On the third column, list the greatest thing this person has done for you. There are probably many, so you must select the single most impactful act they've done on your behalf. Take a moment to really think about it. The fourth column requires the most analysis. In this column, estimate how much energy is consumed with this person as part of your relationship. For example, I have relationships in which we spend 75 percent of our time dealing with their life and 25 percent of our time dealing with mine. I would record this as 75 percent/25 percent. See the diagram below for an example.

Name	Best Quality	Least Desirable Quality	Most impact memory	Percentages (them/me)
Jonathan	Intellectual	Impatient	Help coach and mentor me during a trying time of life	65%/35%
Michael				
Jennifer				
Steven				
Chris				

Life is meant to be lived in groups. I believe this explains why caterpillars travel solo and butterflies travel in groups. The question to consider: Who is in your group? I asked you to perform this exercise because I believe we are all byproducts of those with whom we surround ourselves. Jim Rohn said, "You are the average of the five people you spend the most time with."

At a young and impressionable age, my mother was the first person to teach me love. She didn't teach it to me through words, but actions and deeds. Each person you have listed on your chart deposits something into who you are and how you love. Depending on the percentages, you are either pouring as much as is being poured back (50/50), or one of you are pouring more into the other (60/40). Surrounding yourself with too many people who require more of you than you do of them leads to feeling emotionally drained. Surrounding yourself with people who pour too much into you leads to interdependence. The memory column simply reveals how you remember the person. And the quality columns inform how they help mold you. This is your cocoon. These are the very things which enable you to enter your pupa phase. How you look when you emerge should look eerily similar to at least one of the people on this list in one way or another. In many instances, the least desirable qualities are overcome in each person by your ability to counteract it. If you are truly an average of all five, you could probably add a fifth column and list how you've adapted your personality to match each person on the list.

I believe this is what Shakespeare meant when he said, "to thine own self be true." It's easy to have a chameleon identity. It's tempting to shift and transform to match the crowd you are with. On the contrary, it is difficult to acknowledge and stand firm in your own identity and be a rock other people can build upon. If I go to a pet store and grab a handful of caterpillars in my hand, I wouldn't be able to find differences between them. In contrast, if I go to a pet store and manage to grab a handful of butterflies in my hand, I wouldn't be able to find similarities between them. The butterflies within us were designed to be different and love their appearances. They are true to themselves. They don't give credence to whether they are accepted by society because they are content with who they are, independent of other perceptions.

Throughout my life, several people have poured as much into me as I into them. Each person helped to mold me into the person I am today. Each showed me love. Each challenged me. Each solidified my value system. Each person encouraged me to strengthen my wings and soar like a butterfly. I wouldn't be where I am today without the different people I've encountered along the way. I imagine this explains why the crew members in my second dream all looked familiar. God was preparing me to be patient but informing me I wouldn't be taking the journey alone. Even into the unknown, the relationships I've developed somehow prepared me for each outcome.

Here is my challenge to you: study your chart and determine if you have the right people in your circle. Is the sum of you greater than the sum of those around you? Are you the center of gravity in your world, or do you revolve around someone else? Are you better today because of the relationships you've formed, or do you find yourself in the same situations you were in yesterday? Is there one person who builds you up more than others? These are the questions of the caterpillar within us. Change can be scary when your inner circle is all you have ever known. Without objectivity, it's easy to accept things for how they are because it is how they have always been. I challenge you to look within and be true to yourself.

I came very close to missing my window. Sometime between the time I spent as a young officer in the army and the time I met my wife, I almost settled on a girl who was not my physical, mental, and spiritual equal. She wasn't a bad person. We certainly had good days and bad days like everyone else. She was exactly what I needed at the time. I knew this girl was not meant for me; still, I came close to marrying her just because it felt right. I thought I loved her, but I knew deep within my spirit that if I was with her, God couldn't use me the way He intended. The hardest thing I did up to that point in my life was to turn away from a comfortable life based on the hope of finding my equal.

After the girl and I broke up, I experienced the most difficult period of my life. However, this is the beauty of love: it was in my darkest hours that God showed me the promise of His love. The first sign was sparing my life on the country road when I could have crashed my car into the tree. I received the second sign while working as a General's Aide, a job that challenged me in more ways than I had ever been challenged. That's when God serendipitously presented me with an opportunity to meet my angel.

Anjelica, the love of my life, worked at Rancier Middle School as a dance coach. Rancier Middle School was coincidentally the same school my General attended for middle school. While I was his aide, I accompanied him there to give a speech. As at any other event, my job was to survey the room to ensure I was prepared for any unknown variables that might arise and help mitigate them. My heart was still broken from a bad breakup, and I questioned my struggles with God. I challenged Him months earlier to show me love, since I had such a difficult time finding it myself. Days and nights passed between the first time I prayed this prayer and the day I met my Anjelica. God was always there in the silence, even when I didn't feel His presence.

I spotted Anjelica standing against the wall with her students. I slowly made my way over to her, pretending I was acting in my role as an aide. The General was already speaking, so I couldn't disrupt his speech to make small talk because my job was to pay attention. Still, something inside forced me to try. We started with simple pleasantries. It was difficult to get complete sentences out. She had the most amazing smile, and I simply could not resist the attempt. I couldn't even tell you how we tried communicating without interrupting the General, but it was simply amazing. I didn't want the experience to end. However, as per my usual luck in these situations, before I had the opportunity to exchange contact information with her, another teacher moved between us and started telling me about his time in Vietnam. I usually love to hear war stories, because my father was a Korean War veteran and much of my family served in the military. However, in this instance, I didn't care about his stories. I had one goal, and it didn't start or end with him.

I began to resume the conversation with Anjelica as the General began to wrap up his speech. I was familiar with his cues and knew I was running out of time. I quickly pulled out a business card and wrote, "This is Jon. Maybe we can do lunch or dinner." I also included my cell phone number. Although I hoped she would call me, I didn't believe I had enough time to make a good first impression and expected the worst. As the General and I drove back to base, my text message alert sounded. It was Anjelica. What happened next varies depending on who is telling the story, but since I'm the author, I get to share it how I remember it.

> **Anjelica**: "Hi, Jon. This is Anjelica. This is my number. I'm not supposed to get your number. You are supposed to get mine."

> **Jon**: "Man, I am so glad you texted me. I was afraid you thought I was creepy because I gave you my number without a real conversation."

Anjelica: "I almost did, but I figured I'd give you a shot. I'm okay doing dinner sometime."

Jon: "Well, since you already broke the three-day rule, let's just do dinner tonight."

Anjelica: "Wow. That was forward. Fine. Let's do dinner. What time am I meeting you and where? I am not getting in a car with you without knowing you."

Jon: "Let's do Olive Garden. 8 p.m. If you can't find where I am standing, just ask the hostess to find the man of your dreams."

Anjelica: "LOL! See you there."

Anjelica and I met for dinner at the Olive Garden on the first day we met and stayed at the restaurant for hours. The waitstaff had to kick us out. It was an instant connection. It seemed as if everything I yearned for during those dark days was completed in that one dinner. We covered a wide range of topics and discussions. She was everything I wanted without even knowing I was missing it. Once again, God arrived, this time in the form of an angel, and the opportunity was left for me to choose. I chose love. Anjelica and I got engaged at the same Olive Garden fifteen months after our first date and held our rehearsal dinner there as well. Since the day we met, and over the last ten years, she has been with me every step of the way. She was there every time I emerged from the pupa phase.

She encouraged me to enter the cocoon. In my weaknesses, she has made me strong. In my strengths, she has made me complete. God orchestrated every step along the path which led me to her.

I wholeheartedly believe that had I decided to remain with my ex-girlfriend even one day longer than I did, I would have never met Anjelica. Sure, we might have crossed paths, but I don't believe it would have worked. I needed to be broken. I needed to endure the storms. God needed me to understand that love for myself was more important than love for another. I say this because it was only after I had love for myself that I was able to love another.

The caterpillar within us must evolve before it can become a butterfly. It must remain true to itself during the process. It cannot think it will simply be a butterfly one morning without the evolution. It's all done in steps. The same is true for you and me. We must evolve before we are ready to embrace true love. The only way to evolve is to first accept the wrongs in our lives and embrace opportunities for what they truly are, even if the immediate aftermath is struggle and pain. Love conquers all, and God will not allow His people to suffer a minute, hour, or day longer than His Divine Will requires. He knew exactly what I needed and filled a void deep within my heart.

8

LEGACY: RETURN TO THE MOUNTAIN

When I finally reached the top of Paine Mountain, I sat in quiet reverence of my accomplishment. At just eighteen years of age, I had overcome a major fear. The nautical twilight was upon me, and I began looking down the mountain at all the obstacles I thought I saw. When it was dark on my ascent, sticks looked like trees. Molehills looked like mountains. Branches looked like wild animals. The journey up Paine seemed like a climb up Mount Everest. My perception of reality was skewed, because even after mustering the courage to make the trek, my fear remained.

Every step I took up that mountain diminished an individual fear. With each new step, my perceived adversaries began cheering me on. The deer, which previously dashed in front of me and frightened me, began serving as my guide. The snow I trudged through became a red carpet. The wind that blew in my face shifted directions and began to blow on my back. The stars I saw on the horizon eventually became my light posts. The mountain became my mission. I stopped looking up and began looking down. When I reached the summit, it was as if the mountain was illuminated with heavenly hosts celebrating my accomplishments.

I reached the mountaintop with thirty minutes to spare. I meditated and prayed for clarity and peace. The peace only God can provide. As I patiently waited, the sun began to crest the mountain range. I counted down each minute until sunrise. Not only did I accomplish my first great challenge, but I also planned to see the sun rejoice. Everything went according to my plan. The last order of business was for God to deliver the cosmic miracle. At least that's what I thought. However, something went wrong.

When it turned 6:10 a.m., I began to panic. The sky was lighter, but the sun's rays no longer shined. Clouds quickly overtook the sky. Thoughts began to race through my mind. I did everything right. I packed a day bag. I alerted my roommates where I would be. I prayed. I mediated. I challenged myself. I made it up the mountain. I survived. "Why are there clouds?" I wondered aloud. I asked how I could see my shadow dance if the sky was not clear.

Soon, 6:11 a.m. came. Then 6:12 a.m. The sun was supposed to rise at 6:14 a.m., and I didn't feel peace anymore. Then, it hit me like a ton of bricks. I planned for every detail and every variable. The only thing I forgot to do was check the weather. The local weather forecast for Easter Morning 2004 was overcast, but I was so busy preparing for everything else,

I forgot to check the weather. 6:14, 6:15, 6:16 … The daylight was present, but the sun was absent.

I missed it. The sun did rise that morning, but it did so behind the clouds. God did not intend for me to see my shadow. For a very brief moment, I felt let down. *How could I be so careless?* I felt defeated. But as quickly as the caterpillar reemerged, the butterfly returned and quelled my concerns. I had accomplished way more than I could have imagined on that mountain, even without seeing my shadow. I didn't need time to understand. I didn't need an interpretation of the event. I didn't need to seek counsel. I knew immediately that the old Jon would never have made this trip. I matured, even without the confirmation of God's miracle through the sun. He matured me in other ways. My mission was complete. I began the descent with a great sense of accomplishment.

I journeyed down the mountain singing praises to God and thanking Him for the courage. The real difference on my way back was how I viewed the world. For the first time in eighteen years, I viewed the world with a clear conscience. I returned to campus after several hours and began to share my story. I don't believe every milestone in life ends with a moment of clarity. I tried to explain the journey of self-discovery to my friends, but they couldn't understand. It was my mountain, not theirs. Every caterpillar has its own choice. Every person has his or her own mountain.

I am comfortable with the man I see in the mirror. There are still more phases in life for me. I still have a very long way to go. All I know is I decided at eighteen to begin the metamorphosis. Here I am, some sixteen years later, and I am still seeking self-improvement. Perhaps someday I will return to Paine Mountain on Easter to try again. If I do, I'll be sure to check the weather first. Maybe instead of Paine, I'll choose Everest. Everyone has a mountain. Maybe by the time I am ready for another attempt, my mountain will be different.

I pray that my story touches someone's life in some small measure. I hope that it challenges their inner caterpillar. If I ever met one of my readers, I would tell them to call their caterpillar out to the surface. I would challenge them to acknowledge the shortcomings, fears, bad experiences, and the heartbreaks. I would encourage them to realize that every obstacle is an opportunity for God to show His hand. I would caution them against living their life and dreams as a caterpillar. Instead, I would help them find their tree branch. I would be with them every step of the way as they spin their cocoon and surrender to the world, hang upside, and begin their metamorphosis. I would remind them that the post-pupa version will be superior to the former. The decision to morph must be made selfishly, without regard for the approval of others.

Anatomically, a caterpillar's cylindrical body is incapable of independent flight. While noting this fact and considering life in its alternative, I thank God every day that caterpillars don't fly. I chose not to settle into life. I want more. I want to become a butterfly.

CALL TO ACTION: LAUNCH

Dr. Bill Ramsey told a story about a bad storm that hit a small coastal town. The winds were fierce and the waves violently crashed against the shores. The storm was the worst the townspeople experienced in centuries. When the rain subsided, two friends set-out to walk the beach to assess the damage. They quickly noticed thousands of starfish washed ashore at some point during the storm. The beach was filled with them. Some were dead, but most of them were slowly dying on the shore. One of the guys began grabbing as many starfish as he could and tossed them back into the water. The more he grabbed, the more he seemed to find. His efforts, while well-intentioned, seemed to be in vain.

His friend asked him, "Why are you trying to save these starfish? It doesn't matter how hard you try; it is impossible to save them all. Let the birds feast on the dead carcasses."

Without hesitation, the man responded to his friend while holding one of the starfish, "It's true I can't save them all, but I bet my efforts matter to this individual starfish." He then threw the starfish back into the water and continued saving as many as he could.

After reflecting on the answer, his friend joined his efforts.

I wrote *Caterpillars Don't Fly* because I felt led to parallel my life experiences with the lessons I have learned along the way. I have been blessed beyond measure by God Almighty, and my prayers have been answered. My new prayer is that this book touches someone's heart and compels them to unlock his or her potential. Not just the potential to make more money or find happiness but the potential to be a better person.

I believe everyone at some point was one of those starfish washed ashore and left for dead. The death sentence was not a literal death but rather a sentence to a life of mediocrity. It often takes someone or something tossing them back into the water to present them with a second chance at life- a new opportunity.

Strangely, I imagine each of us have also felt like one of those starfish given a new lease on life. I imagine each reader, at one point or another, wondered aloud how they will pick up the broken pieces of their shattered lives after a storm stripped away all their security. I know I have.

When I sat in my car after purposely driving it into the ditch, I questioned what went wrong. I blamed God for my failures and credited myself for my success. Sadly, that thought left me hopeless at the end of the road. I thought I had it pretty good until a wild storm tossed my emotions, judgment, and securities onto the beach like one of those starfish. However, I needed the storm. I needed God to toss me back into the water. I needed the second chance. Life isn't always about initial success. Life is sometimes about the storm. Success is often measured through perseverance and long-suffering.

One of the most heartbreaking tales of long-suffering I have heard is also a staple for strength and courage. Horatio G. Spafford was a successful businessman in Chicago in 1873. He was a well-respected lawyer and owned real estate throughout the city. His life was complete. He had a beautiful wife and four wonderful daughters to share his success. Even though his young son died two years previously from a bout with pneumonia and much of his real estate investments were destroyed in the great Chicago Fire of 1871, Horatio managed to pick up the pieces and build a dynasty. He knew a vacation was what his family needed.

He sent his wife and four daughters on the French oceanliner, *Villa du Havre*, to England with a plan to join them after he tied up a few business interests in Chicago. As the ship sailed across the Atlantic Ocean, a violent storm tossed it around and caused it to capsize into the water. More than three hundred innocent lives were lost aboard the vessel, including Horatio's four daughters. His wife survived. Heartbroken and devastated, she made it to England aboard a rescue ship and sent a telegram back to her husband in Chicago. The message read, "Saved alone. What shall I do?"

Horatio was heartbroken. He quickly gathered his belongings to recover his wife in England. His family was the source of his strength and the one thing that kept him afloat during the hardships of 1871. As he sailed across the ocean to England, he asked the captain of the ship to notify him at the point where his four daughters lost their young lives. He didn't know what he would do. Perhaps he thought he would get closure knowing the location. Perhaps he planned a brief memorial service to honor their lives.

When the ship arrived at the point, the captain alerted Horatio. Horatio stood silently along the side of the boat and broke down in tears. He didn't understand. He couldn't see past the storm. He lacked the peace of mind he had just weeks prior. He was thrown ashore like the starfish and awaited the death of everything he knew. However, something unexpected occurred. As he explained it years later, a sense of peace overtook him and calmed his spirits. He knew, even at this dark moment, that God would find him and toss him back into the water for a second chance.

In silent reverence, Horatio wrote the lyrics to one of the most powerful songs in the Christian Faith:

When peace like a river attendeth my way,
When sorrows like sea billows roll;
Whatever my lot, thou has taught me to say,
It is well, it is well, with my soul.

This simple declaration went on to become one of the most recognizable hymns in churches across the world. However, few people know the lyrics to the beautiful song were written on a lonely ship in the middle of the ocean while a man cried tears from his soul. Even after all the loss and devastation he experienced, he found a way to declare, "It is well with my soul." Even after Spafford's devastating storm, God provided the peace he needed to pick up the pieces and start anew. This song is sung at countless churches across the world to symbolize peace amidst tribulations- peace after the storm. When my half-brother was murdered in 2005, this song was played at the funeral and it still gives me the peace I need to honor his life today. *It is well, it is well, with my soul.*

Like Horatio Spafford, I believe anyone can be a source of strength for others. I don't imagine he knew his words would affect millions of people, but I do know he wrote what he knew to be true about life and God. My challenge to each reader is to be a source of strength for others. It is my official call to action. I challenge each reader to find a starfish in their life and toss them back into the ocean for the second chance they deserve.

Caterpillars become butterflies through individual choice. However, butterflies survive the metamorphosis through the support of others. I challenge my readers to be the support channel for these young butterflies. Then and only then will they be like Horatio and be equipped to share their story for generations. The Holy Bible records this principle in the book of John 15:13 (KJV), when Jesus proclaims, "Greater love hath no man than this, that a man lay down his life for his friends." I believe this scripture is loosely interpreted to mean "greater love has no one than to aid, assist, and care for the livelihood of their friends and family." Help others be better.

My challenge to each reader is to expand their network of friends and family, to go out of their way to help someone facing similar struggles. To find someone who is walking down a similar path and help lighten their load. To find a mentee or protege and teach them the ways of the world. To bring someone with them to the next levels of promotion and organizational leadership. This is the launchpad. Call it *paying it forward* or *random acts of kindness* or whatever. At each juncture of my life, I learned from someone else who had navigated a similar path and helped guide me through my toughest points. I am better because of them.

As I close this chapter and book, I find myself at another crossroad. This time, I know God has more for me planned. I am no longer satisfied with my current state. Although I attempted to once again take matters into my own hands and route my own journey, I fully accept God's direction. My intention is to ease the load slightly and remind each reader there's a light at the end of their tunnel. Circumstances may not always make sense, but the events in our lives always have a purpose. I'm sure of it. The next chapter I write won't be on paper but in the actionsf I undertake that enable others to unlock their potential. The change, however, won't come from the outside but will originate from within.

I challenge each reader to make a similar commitment. Imagine a world where everyone lives to their full potential.

CPSIA information can be obtained
at www.ICGtesting.com
Printed in the USA
BVHW081438020720
582622BV00007B/34